C000303607

COLLECTED POEMS

First published in 2012
The Dedalus Press
13 Moyclare Road
Baldoyle
Dublin 13
Ireland

www.dedaluspress.com

Copyright © Macdara Woods, 2012

ISBN 978 1 906614 64 5 (paperback)
ISBN 978 1 906614 65 2 (hardbound)

All rights reserved.
No part of this publication may be reproduced in any form or by
any means without the prior permission of the publisher.

Dedalus Press titles are represented in the UK by
Central Books, 99 Wallis Road, London E9 5LN
and in North America by Syracuse University Press, Inc.,
621 Skytop Road, Suite 110, Syracuse, New York 13244.

Cover image © 'Heron and Trout'
gouache on handmade paper, 112 cm x 81 cm
by Poppy Melia
From private collection, New York
Artist's website: www.poppymelia.com

The Dedalus Press receives financial assistance from
The Arts Council / An Chomhairle Ealaíon

COLLECTED POEMS

Macdara Woods

DEDALUS PRESS
DUBLIN, IRELAND

Also by This Author

POETRY COLLECTIONS

Decimal D. Sec Drinks In A Bar In Marrakesh (New Writers' Press, 1970)
Early Morning Matins (Gallery Press, 1973)
Stopping The Lights In Ranelagh (Dedalus Press, 1987, 1988)
Miz Moon (Dedalus Press, 1988)
The Hanged Man Was Not Surrendering (Dedalus Press, 1990)
Notes From The Countries Of Blood-Red Flowers (Dedalus Press, 1994)
Selected Poems (Dedalus Press, 1996)
Knowledge in the Blood: New and Selected Poems
(Dedalus Press, 2000, 2007)
The Nightingale Water (Dedalus Press, 2001)
Artichoke Wine (Dedalus Press, 2006)
The Cotard Dimension (Dedalus Press, 2011)

IN ITALIAN
Biglietto di Sola Andata (Moby Dick Editrice, Faenza, 1998)
Above Pesaro/Con Pesaro ai Miei Piedi (Volumnia Editrice, Perugia, 1999)

TRANSLATION
The King of the Dead and Other Libyan Tales by Redwan Abushwesha,
translated with the author and Orla Woods Abushwesha
(Martin Brian and O'Keefe, London, 1978)

EDITED
The Kilkenny Anthology, with Jim Vaughan (Kilkenny Co. Council, 1991)
Present Tense: Words and Pictures (Mayo Co. Council, 2006)

Collaboration
This time, this place (Mayo Co. Council, 2007)

For Niall – Still Reminding Me

The street sign in Harfleur reads
"Rue Frédéric Chopin – Compositeur
Francais" and then the dates: that's it
et comme ils m'ont fait danser la tête
ces mazurkas ces polonaises
factual cattle-cars rattling East
to the edge of the world in the frost

Son – you must tell them I kept
the hearth-stone sweet
and a clear-burning fire in the grate
please tell them
dis que j'étais invisible
– même imaginaire – should they ask:
let them know I was never a fantasist

ACKNOWLEDGEMENTS

Grateful acknowledgement is made to the editors of the many magazines, newspapers, journals and individual collections in which the poems gathered here, or versions of them, first appeared. 'Unfolding', for Pearse Hutchinson 1927 – 2012, appeared in *Poetry Ireland Review* no. 107.

Grateful thanks to Eiléan Ní Chuilleanáin for making the initial selection and for much else besides.

Thanks to Paul Perry for facilitating the launch of this book at a special event of the Poetry Now / Mountains to the Sea Festival 2012.

Contents

~

Preface

I ARRIVED BACK IN A PLACE I knew well, tired after a long journey, with a perfect anticipatory image of it in my mind, to find when I got there that it no longer existed. The gate, through which I had entered a thousand times, was locked against me, six luxuriant full-grown poplars, which I had seen a few weeks before as airborne silver clouds, lay in their field gutted and filleted, a shady walnut tree now stood hideous, hacked naked as a plucked chicken, and, to round out the absences, an eccentric pine which had leaned astonishingly over the road for generations had vanished as if it had never been.

Which left me, in the gathering darkness, considering the myriad of concurrent realities that whirl around any event. The reality of my remembered image, stored inside my head, clear in every longed-for detail; and then the reality that had been there before my own glittering image was formed; and here too, forcefully pushing its way in, was the urgent new image that my mind was even now in the process of assembling, and the one which the neighbours had presumably already assembled and superimposed in their own minds. And at the same time, while I, (or one of me, in the time-machine in the loft), was clicking the shutter on the instant-to-instant ceaselessly unfolding factual images of the damaged walnut, the stacked poplar trunks, the still locked gate, another *I* was watching the whole process closely and reckoning up the further reality of what all these realities would in turn become. The infinitely reflecting internal mirrors of *nunc fluens* and *nunc stans*.

'The poet is a man' says Thoreau, 'who lives at last by watching his moods. An old poet comes at last to watch his moods as narrowly as a cat does a mouse.'

I believe poets must come to watch their own interaction with the world around them as narrowly as that, even to the extent of becoming part of the watching process. This has nothing to do with self-obsession, but happens because watching, and seeing, is what they have learned how to do. A disciplinary truth repeated at every conscious moment, and probably unconsciously too. The very young, of course, can always leapfrog to the same place by a kind of timeless empathy: There is nothing stable in the world, says Keats, uproar's your only music. I can hear the whine of chain saws through the window behind me as I write this.

I've heard it said that poetry gives life a second chance – both a truism and a marvellous perception. Sadly, because one second chance is really all any of us could bear. And however many years we may have been at it, however much we may or may not have written, whenever we do manage that second chance, that redemption of time itself, it is always partial, a part of the same second chance, or even only the possibility of it, for a moment repeated.

Is this a small matter? Only God can exist in the Static Now, although human kind lay claim to have aspirations. There are poems in this book from more than fifty years ago, the I who wrote them is not the I who reads them today, but we have endless versions of a language in common. Dialects of the body cells, passed on from one lustrum to another, as stories and identities are passed on from one generation to another. Knowledge in the blood. The means by which we live and, for the most part, love.

When Arthur Rimbaud emerged from the barn on the family holding in the Ardennes, with the hard won text of the *Saison En Enfer* in his hand, he first read it to his mother. What does it mean, she is reported to have asked. To which: It means literally and exactly what it says, he is reputed to have replied. Having made these poems there is really very little more that I can, or feel I should, say about them. Eventually simplicity is all, but life becomes more complex, demanding and disturbingly engaging the more fully we live it.

Macdara Woods

March 22nd Meant Love

In turning aside you brushed against
my hands in passing; now sixteen
hours and sixteen days are gone since
I lay fallow before I dared to say
the miracle of love to the riding light
on the ship's high stern.

This ship was built for a journey through
barricades and the waves of your driving
mind, the green brain furled behind
your eyes and the white sail shining
and set to gather stars;

Ambition's turned down crown
shall not touch me; nor dog eared books
nor the murmuring of names in the ten
pin skittled alley of half remembered
childhood tales

Or the tumbling of glass on the barricades:
whisper my name and see them fall to our thunder
and echoing flail, and time in a white rain run
through our high peaked trees.

A bird shall sing in the shadow of your eye,
a single bird in the shining night, a bird
of the dust and the white bone's final breaking
in a wise and wide and stately doom of day.

And Until This

1.
And until this then so
you sat all in all
beneath a willow tree, cool
where the leaves hung over your hair
and the branches held your face.
And I, had I been there
would have held your face
between my hands, or with
my eyes perhaps.
For yes, had I been there
I would await your smile, your
gesture of approval, and then
as sunlight underneath the willow tree
I would make known my want to you

2.
You see these lilies?
I have plucked them for the altar rails,
Unto the rough white lace once
I went, and leaned my chin upon
The cold of marble. Now I bring
These lilies, green and false as gas.

3.
If you have not seen green and silver lights
On city trees, or morning over buildings
Under demon leaves then I would show you
Sleepless streets at dawn and no fantastic
Dawning this: but dawn, cold dawning
Seen in windows
Hungry
And your face grown cold and grey.

Cauchemar Is A White Horse

Wear your hair like a skull cap
burning your brain; lay shoulders bare
like horses to hunger and thirst upon my energy,
for death and disease the offered groin.
One thousand years of horses' hooves
are beating here between twin stars
my eyes: come Cauchemar and ride our nights,
sweat yellow, sweet in the light lifting
from the eyes of Christ crossed in wire
staring in an ivy wind. Come Christ and Cauchemar,
my sweet mares till morning.

Arthur Rimbaud, At Seventeen

At seventeen life is hell
Unless you're a blue eyed bitch
And learn to thumb your feelings well
With a touch of the tensile wrist

And down the unimaginable drinks
Or play the tricks as the tricks are played
Return the rich man's liquid winks
For the piper calls the tune he paid

And the piper pays no easy tune
The gleaming boys must dance
And dance through every jaded room
Satanic figures of romance

The tune is hard the tinsel tears
The fumbling hand must join the round
The rich man doesn't really care
For he has more than poems to spend

At seventeen the choice is clear
Dancing boy or dancing bear
The barman holds the closing rhyme –
The rich man's pulse still marking time

Nor Could The Sea

Nor could the sea have hindered its own two children
walking before and after, though it opened
veil upon veil to the sun of a morning's leaving;
departure, and thus I shall throw no further songs
to the sea's eyes till the sea shall have taught me
the riding of the loose waves: nor will I walk
with love till love shall have taught me need;
nor shall I seek to dress my love in green and red;
and suns shall not drown by my hand.
Instead in these dying days that rivers have clouded
their set souls I shall cut from me what may hold
sunlight or dust so I may live one with the sea grass
and lie with the sea in its coldest shore.

No Birds Took Flight

Believe me now, for in that grey veined dark
I did not understand
Which words were lost, and did not mark
The formal patterns from your hand.

Too real that town and claptrap time
Unmusical but sung;
My words were tossed into a nursery rhyme
Before your ivory dance began.

Each morning cleared the bedroom floor
When only the dead and drunk remained
So gracious a dying that posited more
Or less of death beneath the counterpane.

Forgive me now, for in that leaving so
You loving, dancing there –
(If love were real then love might grow
To a humming-bird in a child's hair)

No birds took flight to flesh or bless
Any whispering word –
Askew in time a hand may jerk and miss
The drifting feathers of a wind-torn bird.

The Drunken Ladies

There was one drunken lady in Dublin
who ginned to sleep and cried
tell me love if we wake in the morning
but the boat had gone, the passage paid,
somebody slipped on the Dublin line.
There were five drunken ladies in Bayswater
the first was a red man's red-haired daughter
or maybe his wife it was no great matter
when four were drunk then one was sober,
there were three drunken ladies in Fulham
who had gone when he went back to London again,
there were two drunken ladies in Paris but
no time to stop to ask their names
for the train was leaving the station and
there was one drunken lady in Spain.

1966 – 1972

From Cyphers One To Five

Cypher 2

1.
I can fly, cried the mad castellan,
See, I can fly like a bat.
And at dawn and dusk he made radar sounds
Flapping his clerical cloth.
I can swim like a fish through the bars
Of St. Peter's tiered tiara;
And then in the evening livid with stars
I hang in the College of Cardinals.

2.
See, I can see, said the poet from prison
As he drew his teeth in the cellar.
So saying he considered the sun as a vision
And quietly cried out on angelic disorder.

Cypher 3

Ice, oh let him have ice for this is fire
This place-name elegy within the mind.

First hand he cries out on the highest power,
Taking shelter in the castles of the Rhine.

Disorder me angels, disordered he cries
Pinned on the graph of Jacob and the Twins;

He has a blood red flower behind his eyes
That whispers outwards through his brain.

Cypher 5

It is spring rain here but time remains
Tuned cold. Gothic cloth in the stone
And Elijah the moonlight admiral drowns
In the sliding years for none catch hold

Spring tide, neap tide; seasons lead on
For this one sailor who saw most clear
As when Elijah, the fabulous charioteer
He drove witch-haired down see-saw roads
Declaiming through eyes of water-glass
His three-card summer time pleasure boats
The cordage learned and the master rigged
To keep his ship-of-line loves afloat.

Deliver him this much Norse lady now
A white chart for return; how might he go and how
Re-engage with his terrible moons of war
For he fears their sharp and riding shapes,
In the pumpkin world their lanthorn teeth
Are spilling his dreams from mouth to mouth,
Who moves forever through an agony of wakes
To beach, a tendril mandrake of the rocks.

It is spring rain, yes, but time remains
And Elijah turned in the stone.

Prologue

London London – it is night-time and white
In this return from fantasy through time;
A boat's span of ocean and an ocean of wit
I've travelled again and left my sense behind
          with
My first green fields and my white-haired girl
In the towns where she rose to me dark and fair;
And I'm paring the light in a private return
Extending the shadows of reason and despair
          here
For winter is perhaps the time for thought
Since I've grown afraid, aware of death;
A time to lay some old subversive ghosts
By ritual and bone, walking the night to walk
          off
Demons; witches and physicks now count the cost
Of all who fingered in my lode of treasure
For a charm of trees, and let the dead air loft
Their measure of the springtime forest's measure.
          Meath
I shall answer; my country and town and time,
Green and distant that childhood of trees
When each river could quench my distortion of mind:
Surely such seasons are worth some elegies.

Third London Nursery Rhyme

I am working, my love, in Clapham High Street
Spinning my hours to a weekly wage
Weaving my scheme in an English workshop
And singing by times of the nights and days

For this is the limited tumble of choice
If ever you leave the wilderness bed
To run with the hare and tear with the dog's jaw
Function as living, and cheaper than dead.

Still, singing by times of the nights and days
For light must splinter where love will dawn
Despite the backslapping crackle and praise
That gleamed in the years of the poetry bums

When we were too young, and being young believed
That love was the charm for the loveless day
O the quick man leaped and our truth he thieved
And he scattered us out upon every way –

Run out of town for speaking of love
And sharing a bed to support the word,
For that being lovers we still could grieve
And grieving pray want be a misericorde

Our laser of mercy to ice our world
From the decked-out gleeman's ritual graph
Of poetry damned footsteps dutifully hurled
Down the abandoned apache paths.

Now it's time to remember, remember they pay
The cheques and the debts for the dancer must live
But the tambourine dancer will dance away, for
Grey is the colour of the coin they give.

Controlled And Intermittent Falling

I'm sailing my hoist 15 stories up
watching the truth through a chink in the boards
a piece of dislodged concrete turning slowly
like a lazy killer-fish in water sinking down
the levels of floors – And if you were to ask I'd say
my circles of experience spiral in
like a zoomshot on a staircase –
dizzy to look up and dangerous to look down.
What wind will form me patterns now,
eccentric circles, fragments of stone?
Unless the dancers and the strangers
who refuse to get it straight
the legend on my doorway reads
London: Cul de Sac.
Turning the wheel by opposites they sharpened steel
for a punctured lung on a railway bridge,
an eye gouged out and sepsis from a dirty knife;
the houses shrinking on a razor's acid edge,
arterial roads, two rooms, a telly set;
Thursday noon, pay packets and perhaps a bet,
Guinness and Bitter – the leering Black and Tan –
offense, surprise if you object;
thing is that we were doing our best
to keep a troubled ship together
on bad sea-roads where each port seemed
less likely than another.
A tree in Green Park must make do for a forest
a pool set in mortar make do for an ocean
a street full of windows must make do for sand dunes,
the one action open is captive; is walking
without speaking, without stopping, without turning:

and so, from fifteen stories up
some lives become apparent. A definition:
controlled and intermittent falling.

Lavender Hill

It's not too many years till they all vanish down
To the cold of the moon from the heat of the sun

Pushing a pram where no children have been
And leaving her tanners in the fruit machines
Sixpenny Annie on Lavender Hill has
More truths to tell than she has time to kill

And Sidney the Gnome comes bicycling down
By the Queen of Castille into Wandsworth town
Where the sad Duke of Cambridge locked in his head
Says Jones shut up shop, take the bookie to bed

But Miss Jones the ailing newsagent maid
Waits for the words which have never been said –
When peace is the conflict, peace by decree
In the peace fallout, slowly – O who will have me,

Sees the quick boys in Clapham – fame is the ton –
And the writ-waving landlords waiting to dun
On the door of the teahouse, The Pakistan Moon,
Are the star of the occident later or soon

It's not too many years till they go underground
As deep as was buried and never was found

Poor Sailor who waits for the call from the grave
Swears to fifty bad years since real ale was brewed
He tightens his life belt and says on the blink
You sups four or five pints and you ain't 'ad a drink

While Muscles in panic on Battersea Bridge
Cries four thirty two there's an hour left to live
The French Lady slides away out on the tide
With ten purple dogs and the devil inside

And Jim Fish the baker admits that he's scared
His hands shake so badly he can't shape the bread
But latched to a standard, traversing the rough,
He laughs tap a new barrel one's never enough

For the man in the moustache awaiting his friend
Who is keeping and holding his shattered left hand
But there's no fear of dying no sound of a song
And we all need an anthem to play out the end

The Snow That Scatters The Leaves

The snow that scatters the leaves in London
Drives lean, but strips no leaner than
The wind that rattles the bones in Dublin

Where the hope that marks the heart in time
Razors its legend, inlays it by wind
In the incestuous lithograph Irish mind

And dazzles to flower in the Dublin tongue –
An urban tongue for an easy song
That dragonflies time into thistledown –

But if time is thistledown time is thorned
As the harmless joke is barbed,
As the seaward jerking river rides and daubs

The city's silt on its morning walls,
Salvation etched along the water-front
Each seabird's gay-day trip to dare night fall.

Morning is the commerce of escaping the town
The boat the knife the wake the word,
But court and justice need tumbler and clown,

The tangled knot is a withered cord,
The best-known truths are never learned,
And departure is mockery prefiguring return.

So the Dutchman returns back, early or late,
Though canvas rot and pitch-pine burn
If you sail by the compass you sail with fate,

And it's virtue of want makes the black ship run
Forever for the landfall light,
And love is the power of the stripped bones

That pierce the sun and drive through night
For the touch of a word
A word to secure their uncrucified flesh.

Image word and truth, these at least have been
My own, I did believe
And inhabited fine fantastic scenes,

I said love is made when the song is begun
As I slipped through the liquid city then,
And a woman loves best who loves but one

Or spins through her life in a riddle of men,
Rehearsing the cities of the plain,
And laughs in the grey-faced arc of the sun

Till the dream and the arc converge again
And rise to confront the ethical man
On his tightrope night time journeying home.

For she and hers have best informed
Through dark and day the talisman,
Their heart's belief the fragile charm

To dissolve the riddle of catch who can,
And the problem bared is perennial return –
Prepaid cost of remembering.

Through the end of season air the wise birds cry
Wise since they may leave
And singing grieve to tell wherefore and why.

Go Back, Go Back, said the guinea fowl in the garden
Oh the green-leaved trees grow small –
Memory is tempered now filed and sharpened

To burst asunder the garden wall
Go Back Go Back to the shrunken garden –
The child's most final growth of all.

My ring-toed women each time affirm
That memory always calls half-heard
Through the shadowy glass of the backroom mind

What you doubt by dark you will regain by day
And working on until the song is made
Drive through wonder to the poem

To the quiet depth where the unknowing guide
Still murmurs over your going,
That old man trembling in a whitewash room

For the burning thirst that blocked his throat,
And how I remember him.
One bright spring day the dust clouds rode

The sun and dried his winter basement room
In the Roneo's ironic hum
Until only the furtive thirsty eyes remained

Alive and looking through his panic found
Between him and the workday clock
Long desperate years of loss and dust.

Though he rear up memory, his arms outspread,
So easy to bypass him and his kind –
Polite evasions confidently made

Nothing to fear from steel-trap jaws,
No unconsidered word would fall
No thread of pity dangle in the mind.

But forgiveness lies in remembering him
Remembering all the drunken men
If only for the grief of what we may become

When thrust outside the green-leaved garden,
A passage that must be made
To those stone streets where the red heart hardened

Set for survival learns to trade
Off all the fragile odds and ends of thought
We carry along the way

To try to rebuild the garden wall
To straighten the branches most misshapen
And stay for a while the dead tree's fall.

The Dark Sobrietee

In the confines of the public park
and the blooming of sandragon trees
I met a fair haired woman
who said soldier follow me
Ah then no my love I answered
for I know love's company
they would fix me and fact find me
in the dark sobriety

By the confines of the ocean
and the serpentining sea
I met a dark haired woman
who said sailor sail for me
Ah then no my love I answered
there are seven riding seas
and the course is reckoned dead dear
by the dark sobriety

In the confines of the city
and the evening flying free
I met the rarest woman
who said poet follow me
Ah then no my love I answered
I have prayed and drunk the lees
and what's left me now is searching
for the dark sobriety

The Sixteenth Kind of Fear

Who was it moving the curtain then?
Only the wind, the hand of the wind.

And who was it making light dance in the wind?
Only the sea-light caressing the sun.

Who was that walking when night came down?
Just a night-watchman thinking of home.

And whose was the face at my mountain window?
Only a dead tree white as a bone.

Whose was the fever then, cold in the sun?
Only my love's when my love lies alone.

And who is the stranger I meet in the evening?
Only the future, love, coming and going.

Just A Private Pilgrimage

Strategic grey birds rose up from the roots,
flew shale-eyed in sunrise across the rocks
of our Mexican, our coffee-and-brandy-bonded mountain
over Clew Bay and County Mayo.
I mean the pilgrim church looked Mexican
and lost for a drifting Western hero, though
it held its foundation in bog and rock and rain;
in public barefoot suffering between the shrines
and stalls and cups of tea and water urns.

A compliment. I don't know really what I mean,
for we've been blown adrift like leaves on railway platforms
between the rush and vacant spaces of the trains:
Clapham Junction, Clapham North; in Mortlake, Richmond,
    Cheam,
in opaque London morning time. Red brick, black stone
and sliding streets. Nothing much remembered
but the names: thank God the chart is lost and gone.
But still, I was aware
with some few friends in the public parks
that the countess slept-afar –
in dark and light in Leeson Street
bedraggled flowers and tangled hair

First Letter For J. S.

Now if I had been wise then maybe I would make
A marble bell for you to toll the world

Across this doubting dog-watch lake of words. But
Sceptical as ever was – derisively unsure and frail

I am not wise and never was but something does remain
For I do hold some circuits in the mind, a wind

Whereby I can believe in different kinds of pain.
Listen though, geraniums bloomed in Lavender Gardens

When all your leaping words were said; eternally
Within that loss of sound your sorrow sharpened

All remembrance of the less than dead. The heads
Upon the balcony, the dipping heads of swans combined

With Leda and with lovers and with memory and mime.
But then I had no answer and so surely was not wise.

Come dance with me – you said – or could you dance
Or could you, dancing with me, redeem time? But

You knew I could not step into your anguished eyes
Without some fitting song or symbol to explain

Why I have such dependance upon such ruin of rhyme.
Could I reduce complexity and tell it to you plain.

Decimal D. Sec. Drinks in A Bar in Marrakesh

Diminishing perspectives but these of sound
mixed like the pigments of his hand
and out of green and swivelled eyes
the white guide leans and shuffles tongues.
A bright bazaar he operates
and nightly glides through shapes.
Some phrases, yes, of English
(Decimal I'm speaking of the ratings)
"you like my yellow slippers or do I introduce" –
the choir of fallen angels in the fallen loft
lift up the paper curtain of the smoke,
nod sometimes sideways and give voice –
"you like my pretty slippers" and his voices crack
in circles; but never mind, his eyes are bright
while gloved in black his mind climbs up
until in triumph (pause) he then replies
(who asked the questions voices far apart)
– yes red – yes black – and I keep count.
Ah Decimal: five live fowl make up a hand
a bottle of chilled water and a glass of wine
and no you cannot play without the knave
who fumbles words with his sliding mouth –
so guard your cardboard fingers on the page;
the knave in truth though not the ace
is upside down; is curious and high.

Jadis si je me souviens ...
thinks Decimal crossing the Djemaa el Fna
"... and sable lady how I thought
that I had found my countess there
a brocade lady in a bar

whose mouth could counterpoise her stare
and split monopolistic chatter."

And Decimal! I swear
not one, but many nights he prayed
his friends arrive
Ah qu'ils viennent ...
and he might make a statement, undismayed.
"How should I care of time –
wise men make mistakes,
and dead men plague my breath
and some who make a planned campaign
still end up crimson in the groin."

The green and yellow dust that rises from her palm
my countess, broken silver in a shape
still makes though false a very fair alarm
and through her eyelids tells me to escape –
capuchins, capes or sandals,
plainchants, Gregorian interludes perhaps
Gueliz – the church; l'eglise
without the walls, without words perhaps
and the grand and sunlit situation
of a stranger's greeting
in his quietly stated question –
most courteous ... "you've had a glass of wine?"
My lady countess flies out seeking room
and sunlight falls down drowning felled by incense
inflamed by daylight – bullets criss-crossed in the sun
asquint in mid-week afternoon
Decimal moves through the cedar wood
– red wool clacking on the loom –
and arm in arm they stroll among the souks.
"You like my terracotta city or should I introduce
of black Americans dancing

of red magicians and fruit
of night-time; hiding passports
painting chessboards
of doves and colours and a frail glittering glass of smoke."

And all of this so simply re-echoed
on not more than three grace-notes
is hardly the same as the snakes that glisten
or the tourists that glisten
and wise men, Doctors and Dentists of the Place
the rich people in the French Quarter
all cottoned and neighboured in fractured syntax
or subterranean irrigation
or the sun astray in the chessboard
of queens, bishops and impenetrable thorns
that borders the town.
Decimal, hand on heart would say
"If you have not found the end
in the grey point of the briar or
the edge of blood that plumes upon the mouth
or dries or dies in any such escape
do not read your sophisticated books by sunlight
and: if you must drink beetroot juice as wine
then beware of honey and nuts."

A pause. Then
evening, daylight and the pipes are out
— there is some husbandry among the dead —
the Artistic Angels of the Place hang fire
and the waters of the Atlas are cold as blood.
Decimal, communing with glass histories
glass smiles glass walls glass roofs
says yes, we have a need, but not of evidence or proof
for, reaching in his pocket

I saw the selfsame barman give
some of my money for grace of alms
and watched
while the same bar clock slowed down.
Twelve thirty five
and time to move to find the threshold of her eyes
– knock three times and ask for halwa –
she'll maybe offer honey too for after all
three painted pictures make a plate –
a grey illumination. Listen:
Item: "Where we come from it rains
sometimes black and sometimes blue
and the opaque crystal of the sky comes down
like the touch of a policeman's arm
and money is often as tight as here and there
one cannot always dine off sunlight."
A pause. Then
evening, daylight, morning now –
so much has vanished overboard, so many
smiles and eyes and figures of the night:
and all such tourist information
barely co-exists
with so much concrete unreality
of histories and politics –
Berber warlords of the Atlas
sent underground behind the walls
by accident of history
and fate
El Hadj El Glaoui
sometime Eagle of the Atlas
Black Panther
and Pasha of Marrakesh.

So: "sable lady see how he needs
as well as storks upon the walls
most sacred and quizzical
or crescent moons and stars
on the waters of the Aguedal
where a Sultan drowned
in a drowned tree's grip,
as much as this see how he needs
the morning sea-light on the lakeshore

where he could make the journey of his eyes
and find Ophelia asleep among the reeds"
sang Decimal sang Decimal sang Decimal

Shará Bab Rob
Marrakesh, January/February, 1969

Curriculum Vitae Coming Up To Twenty-Seven

I am a pipefitter's mate and I have my cards to prove it
and I paid my union dues
when I worked on the Bunny Club in London, and possibly
scalded the tails off half the bunnies in London
but, I put the heating in, & I wrote a poem.

I demolished a bank in Golders Green
but I did it like God from above
only I used a fourteen pound hammer and a pick
– I was absolutely legal –
so I didn't get such a good return, but I wrote a poem.

I was a postman in Coventry,
they said it's ten pounds a week for one round a day
and I said, right I'll manage two
and I did and I lasted a week, but
I'm a good postman, & I wrote a poem.

I planted trees in the West for Ireland
cleared twenty acres of bog with my friends –
planted twenty thousand Sitca spruce by hand –
and that was voluntary so I wasn't paid at all
but I'm a forester, & I wrote a poem.

I worked on the building sites in Paris
drove a drill through concrete and the language
but I never acquired a labour permit
so maybe in the end we can't count that
but I worked my passage, & I wrote a poem.

I was a milkman on Putney Common,
the foreman was a ballroom dancer
though he didn't dance much with his bottles of milk,
from five in the morning till four after noon
and then I went home, & wrote a poem.

I was a gipsy in Hereford
picking hops for brewing beer
and worked in the sulphur of the drying kiln
for an extra thirty shillings a week,
slept in a cattle truck, & I wrote a poem.

I admit I was lazy in Marrakesh
I didn't work, no, I just wrote poems
but now I'm nearing twenty-seven
I think I'd like a small back payment;
please send me something on account.

Carrillon Appeal

Mayhem and murder
say the bells of disorder

It is an affliction
say the bells of addiction

But not without merit
say the bells of true grit

I will own it my own
say the bells of renown

Ten in each hundred
sing the bells of investment

And would you then let me
ask the bells of upset me

Or maybe you'd leave me
say the bells of believe me

Oh leave you I shall not
says the sad bell of found out

Decimal's Early Morning Matins

He sang upon a roof top
in a crooked afternoon
(Dear Eve, and song, dear evening
such shadows saw him hung)
"If I were only half the ghost
of the ghost you thought heard sing
you'd know before you sold me short
Black Shadows take some time."

And Eve unlocked her eyelids;
disbelieving asked him in
across the intervening streets
of the web that held him down
(misshapen though his fingers were
they fastened on the sun)
and she called "think before
you come to me
Black Shadows take some time."

A shuttered neighbour at her window
saw his hand's grip falter where
the cock-crow of a sundial
was triumphant on the air.
And Eve, behind her casement,
calm as snowflakes snapped the line;
and falling is so gentle and
Black Shadows take some time.

Memory Of Joan

Six taxis in rhythm
traversing the city
the lids of the boots
swung up and swayed down
in the first sat the mourners
with a half-pint of whiskey:
she spoke of madonnas
and paid for the wine.

Six taxis in rhythm
not merely her fancy
the gulls were a cortege
on O'Connell St Bridge,
there was no one in crepe
it was action, excitement
strung tight as a drum
by a dead daisy chain.

Six taxis in rhythm
went crawling through Dublin
I took my departure
at the brown water's edge;
six taxis in rhythm
moved down the horizon
like ravens preceding
the final bare stage.

Carboneras

Carboneras
was a candle in the window
of the scaffold before Africa;
Christmas sunlight touched the stones,
mozaics, and white-washed houses.

Carboneras
was wine in the morning,
black suits and early, guilty brandies
– a disregarded gipsy's warning
against expected laughter.

Carboneras
was also fearing red mountains
yet lacing your boots and walking
through fields of no heather
in the dower-house meaning.

Carboneras
was the crack of something breaking
or about to break in the season's ending.
Or perhaps, one day, just a place to remember
as the port of some soul's landing.

Lassailly

Didi and thanks, look here are
somnambulists, fakirs, mountebanks
conversing in circles (no great harm
by times – more like warmth I
think) somehow a nineteenth century design.
Balzac, flambeaux and trousers of swanskin;
anxious and homeless, some roads lead home.

Dear Souls In September

Dear souls; let me say this
"Thank you all a lot" and yes I know it is
about time we finally got here but
I'm afraid necessities of time delayed us.
Anyhow we took ourselves
a boat among sea-gulls and sailed in a shut-in bar,
disembarking was awakening, our expedition
among cloisters of walls. And in the morning
when the sun sees fit to circle round once more
we'll find ourselves a white curved road
above and over yonder and sing a song,
or tell a story, do a dance or make a poem.

The Burning Tree In The Public Gardens

The burning tree in the public gardens
Shocks, like seeing the swaying of curtains,
Blue smoke whirling in no wind,
And the flame of that tree in a half-lit bedroom
Would terrify. Sunlight or shade. No tree remains
But the image on the retina is scratched and stained.

Destruction of a childhood picture is mainly
Reduction of things, the deck-chair in Stephen's Green
Is an ass and cart on a Georgian roof.
The ambuscades of Tiger Lil and Tiger Moth,
The great tall ships,
Cigarette cards of the First World War,
Are all gone to ground with my Grandfather's hand
That led me by times up Pembroke Street.

I remember too the whistling of trains
When I slipped from a wet verandah onto the rails
And I called in a child's voice *Granda I'm safe*
With the green balloons that float with seagulls
And beside the convent on Leeson Street
Pigeons sang in the tower of the church
And paid no tax on their black-framed windows
But coiled like lovers around the struts.
Until the church was razed for a building site
And their throats were silenced by builder's lime.

And now when I see the tree aflame
The thought is a constriction in the chest,
Grey ash on a poised cigarette, erect at an angle,
Between concrete fingers,

Belabouring what might have been.
In a tumbling of fiery wood the sparks
Are red and yellow phantoms in the dark.
The gombeen and goad are tearing down my childhood,
Not brick by brick but roof by stack,
And leave me watching at the age of thirty
In the perfect teeth of these buildings a graveyard gap.

Rosbeg, July 2nd 1970

The mouth is open, taste awash,
The raw wind howls upon the roof,
scythes the soldiering nettles,
and dark drives boats to fear and sea.
The road bends; two nuns approach me
under a stern St. Joseph's stare
(while wire will hymn without benefit of clergy)
and, we smile, then pause for civil greeting:
"a shop?" "yes Sister, down the road"
& I'm treading the eggshell path for a drink.

I find a cadence in this countryside
-- washed white flat Japanese light;
the straight haired figures of a yellow print –
and so I'm nearing happy, though I can't decide
whether it be rock, or space, or wind
that filters through the mind.

The Dark Between The Days

ONE
The waterspout rears itself as snakes, and sways,
its last dim shore recedes
in the charcoal four-run tide between the days
for an unstocked journey. No harbour or night-light these
tumescent suns; but the acid bites flesh; light stars
they flash; flash back, and stab in the liquid dark.
The combat sergeant in the mess is armed,
Jim Hawkins in the rigging calls for Israel Hands,
a boy and a girl sleep beneath stairs,
somewhere a private is clutching his groin
and woodsmoke licks through the garden.
And so the memory: dividers protract, enclose,
a faint smell of apples on the cold kitchen floor
(the boy and the girl sleep under the stairs)
and spike the walls and rip the starfish chart.

That kitchen-garden door will never open;
tonight the probing finger finds the heart.

TWO
is simply this;
it's about a year since I gave you a poem,
remember: "Balzac, flambeaux, and trousers of swanskin"?
somehow canal water learned to intervene. Panic
and ratchets and wheels on the sombre locks
froze in my mind on my morning walks; not least
the winter image of the dead horse in the park.

Somehow Iaachus became a boon companion
in all last summer's trembling days
among the hospital garden's dried up trees
Leeson Street, Stephen's Green, the stretch to Portobello
but you had the long dark summer in nightshade.

The Goddess Rhea cured him of his frenzy
but left me mine as I sat in the college library
Jean de la Wod, John from the Woods you might say,
means Mad John (Mad Sweeney) or a dried-up leaf.
How then could I compose a poem –
I cannot yet compose myself.

THREE
Panthers on the mantelshelf
transfix me with their eyes and so begin
the haul of dark between the days

the innocent blank page that kills

and in this night do I, could I
remember Paris green? Green women from
the underground

an adolescent Proserpine

not boasting now of ships or heavy seas.
A simple chance of dice I throw
on rattan matting in a metro shelter

Encolpius is beaten to his knees

cough the call – "ten drops of blood
nine blue nails in the sexton's door"
such English words I think remembered

the listing street is waterlogged

and the cross strut of a window frame
plumes like a dancer's fan. Dark between
the days, I feel

such loving drives us on

FOUR
was that blue light of morning
the grass by the window growing and greening,
the angry black midge and the clag-fly eating
cattle and horses, and the dirt road shimmering;
the bogland was heavy and the morning rising.

And you and I for the daylight waiting
in Old Time's Castle Keep,
for terror heard, the first bird waking
sounding the knell of oblivion or sleep;
the bogland was heavy and the light was rising.

The mountains moved through their arcs to speak
"Little you know of the valley spaces
if our insistence could offer you fear
no tree, no bush, nor aught of shelter
will you find in your restless walking here."

Across the candles our eyes were shifting
in dread of the blue-veined window pane,
each morning demands another confronting
for sooner or later you must face time.
But the land is easy and heavy lying
          expectant in the morning's rising.

Decimal's Liberal Schooling, And After

Human in deed his mentors were
when first our Decimal drew breath
upon the flies that circled on his sight
and he learned to speak in chords;
strange indeed and dressed in black
(the evening star presages night
and Decimal is frightened of the dark
his birth-card is the ace of spades)
and so, at last, North Africa,
he recognises basilisk, remote, mosaic
in the columned city of Volubilis,
Alexander Helios and Cleopatra Silene
most ancient sun and moon as twins smile back
and the dark ace winks up gently from the pack
though touched and greased with finger marks
still such as opened many feasts. A stranger
near the heart and two red kings at the door
crab claws scuttle and clutch and
Decimal runs through the streets in fear
for though in fact he's well informed
he reaches out an empty hand ... and so

Black gentlemen in wings of black, he cries,
now give me something more than dust or chalk.

Four Precepts

1.
My woman wild in warmth has died
Alone in the cold sea towns
When the sea scattered her limbs wide

Late and naked she found
The lost shore of her body's pride.

2.
He who would be saint must dare
First the withering of youth,
And wandering strip love bare
To the teeth of his heart's truth.

3.
Mad woman to the young,
When she spoke with a wry mouth
Her words were strong

But when she turned south
From her heart's town,
Truth poisoned her tongue.

4.
When the raven first courts love
My love shall die to the black north bird,
Four cold seasons in the heart
Have taught me the sense of her words;

Four cold seasons in the heart broke earth
And the flame of the frost
Burned in her soul till her body scorched
In the dead fields of her youth's dust.

Credentials, As It Were

Five weeks upon the mountainside
crying in the solar wind –
something occurs in November –
it's poetry today and my feet are on fire
on fire my love again:
punctuating the mackerel roads. The
stroboscopic eyes of cars, the stares
no longer graze – a standard exercise
and I no longer fear the cold eyes.
The drowned water gives off air
for islands floating down the tide,
the limit of endurance is not to be afraid –
but to move onward as the gulls ride.
Then should I follow horseriding clouds
to the unicorn well where morning breaks?
Following down the curlew paths
to where the lost wind waits. O state
a destination Countess: call the stakes
upon the green baize table-land,
the cards are turning in the railed box
and I don't hold the joker in the pack –
though maybe healing fingers might unlock
the sunlight at the mind's back
old lizard brain
and bring me safe beyond the rocks.

Mater Misericordiae, Eccles Street 1971

October the sixteenth late in the evening
the lungs of the trees ordain;
the crab, the begonia, the tight-avised mollusc,
are points in the landscape's change.

Once it was evening
coloured by vineyards
a bright yellow bottle
deep in my pocket

Calmly we walked through the dead mimosas,
the skeletal flowers insist –
the broken shoes and the rag and taggle clothing
for a journey that should have meant Greece.

Once it was evening
a dark sea was rising
the blood of the wine-skin
freckled my throat

Near the Virgin's Chain we slept on the hillside –
the Gorge of Verdun demands
flesh for its bracken, the first teeth of winter,
the church bells were far distant islands of sound.

Once it was evening
a red bird was screaming
the heat of the cognac
was sun in the mouth

October the sixteenth late in the evening
the rules of the game obtain;
when I moved like a spider weaving my footsteps,
instinctive I carried no blueprint or plan.

And now it is morning
the sea has receded –
cold weight of the shoreline
that crushes me in

Release Papers

Late October and I'm out
on a fair day you might say for Dublin
but a cold day for the breeze block Qasbah
down at the bottom of the garden. Its
lizard eyes thin slits of light
for the sun to hide in corners.
Kennedy's snug is shaped like a ship
time and the clock collide
forever taking each other to task
and smoke, like a sluggish anaconda,
recoils and glides on polished glass.
A fair day you might say, for a market,
or driving heavy beasts to the buyers
along the first rime-frost of the roadside.
So much for reality: the warm smell of cattle,
thick coats hot whiskies and ash-sticks
prodding the side-stepping bullocks.
So much for late October and the season,
a cruel five month journey into March
and the frozen fields all scorched of shelter
as the clock and the year run down.
La Grande Armée crosses the stubble land
as the teeth of a harrow rake,
black horses cross the window panes,
glacial patterns, Cossacks in the shape
of scald crows scrabble on the make.
Pinioned in winter the question is
year's beginning or season's end?

1973 – 1986

A Sea of Rooves & Leaded Gables

A sea of rooves and leaded gables
made me feel easy in Paris
each in its way infamous as Casanova's
and each as much battened down; cone
upon cone in the morning, segmented,
opening on racy lines of washing;
on lives (garlic and gauloises climbing the air shaft
clearly misnomered a courtyard)
and the triangular shapes recede
becoming a morning-fluffed pigeon
or a blue boy whistling his way to decision –
the Lycée and rancour of leather.
The wine was good and the bread still better
though both remained from the night before;
hot coffee, cheese and apples on the parapet,
we hung like a bell in the frame of the building,
imaginary wings averted vertigo
and the curtains swung like a metronome.
In the night we flecked our eyes with sequins
and watched the yellow drops cascade
of Pernod poured in candle-light
and laughed and made love unafraid.
Waxlight wanes to morning; shapes remain
a brown ankle caught like a bird in the coverlet
an arm crooked lazily amain
two tangled bodies: les jeunes gens
en numero dix, Hotel du Commerce
Rue de la Montagne Ste. Geneviève
and poems on the tiles like stains.
Trigonometry of course has rolled the bones –
would I at such distance know you again?

Not in mimosas nor pine-trees nor bamboos
not in the forest of the Ardennes
not on the geranium road to Alicante
not in the cornfield near Boulogne
not in the Berkshire haystacks we slept in
nor Dover Beach nor any ship's pitching –

In one place only perhaps I might find you
among walls and scree on the western seaboard
in the spray half-blinded atop Dun Aengus
if your lips were salt
and your smile were anxious
as under the willow you once smiled approval
for it is not just time, love, that drove in the wedge.

Falling Down Borges' Stairs

This is the step that is conjointed
with a joist somewhere in the sinking house;
despite its symmetry is out of true
a perfect image of a battle-field, anonymous
and sometime after bare of trees
that bloomed and burgeoned on the hessian coloured map
(curled edges on the camp-site table top,
the lamp asquint – light slanting from the left
corners held down by cigars and shells and lead)
& the nostalgic wind-blown wafts of paraffin
such as fill the white nights, water and cognac,
the soot that smudges on the tent,
& the Emperor, secure within his tunic, nightly
must decide with stabbing index finger
which companies he must deploy, what hooves will mark
the paper with upturned symbols of good luck –
the same that turn the race-course upside down;
the Louis d'Or that ride upon a jockey's yoke
tumbling askew between sky and earth.
The Equestrian School and the forge present
for him, for me, not much – perhaps a moment
just before the choice; one could retreat, retrench,
before experience of second thought. My
foot upon the stairs is led forever down
these blood-mottled steps; mirrored in sabre and boot

For Jack Walsh d. London 1973

No, it does not surprise me that men die
but that they live so long against all odds
and, running their fingers on the table learn
again the splinter points of braille, the bark
of trees grown brown and bent long journeys past;
a name in lacquer on a box,
across the years, across the years; all chaff.
Forgive me; I have not forgot your foreign city garden
nor gravel paths, your cypress trees,
the endless exploration of your petrolled weeds;
I know the cells, the bones, the fluid of the brain,
you, drying frayed electrode that tumbles in the ground
and in the earth seeks out the waning moon –
& old friend I'll welcome-in each deep new year
and eat the speed and flash of sap and root,
take home the wound of sunlight from the stone
and pray your present river air and reed be keen;
as mine, your best works stand unfinished …
spring time and autumn, a circle of bright roads

Oh God deny me not the time to learn my own design –
an old man in blue evenings beyond the fear of windows
who answers clearly through the falsity of lines
that life is, is glorious, and flawed. Not polished;
undiminished.

Derryribeen, Westport, June 16th 1975

I pray you peace, you household gods
while daylight lasts, and the globed lamp burns.
Today with trowelled hands I picked
mortar from between the bricks;
dust of years on your packed earth floor;
congealed; new smoke from the sunken grate
stormed like Djinns through the wall,
fingered a lapsed corner of the thatch;
your gallery three oleographs, a pope, two saints,
and good enough for Greco's ecstasies.
This cruel toothed trowel proceeds
along the surfaces, the crevets, the edge of stone
interstices – I come upon a hollow place –
a rooted, peasant, catacomb,
and here, I see, you hid your folded hair,
the seasoned clippings of your nails,
pathetic, nameless, but remembered etceteras
all marked collect.
I offer you no hurt & nor do I disturb, distract.
This evening, quiet as sleeping trees,
household gods; I pray you peace.

Cassandra Speaks About The Irish Famine

Give me that sharp knife, the butcher's cutlass
that shall lacerate your womb,
do not endear me when the knives are sharp
do not sleep easy in your homes;
by times the night-winds slip in easy
and occupy your beds
the dead horse and the dead rider
are threatening your gods. What distaff
could you offer in the compound – ha –
would it even matter – a whiff in the nostril –
I speak of blood and of a universe that couldn't listen:
there is blue-stone in the mountains
in spring rivers gold glitters
think before you make a time of rags and flitters
& hand me that sharp knife, the butcher's cutlass,
better to cut out the sore
than die, begotten, eating reeds in ditches

A Leather Tourniquet She Asked

Those Egyptians knew their teeth
caries and cavities
and the mythological road from Rathgar
(bottles of stout and boxes of matches)
slung in their lantern jaws;
two thousand years, I ask you,
the mummied fossil answers to the X-rays
combs back its yellow hair from brow
and reaches hands across the centuries –
incipient messages from me to you;
clickety-click it's (static) six six six
and God alone knows who comes through the door
this time. Blue eyes upon a dot
upon the microfilm of the ages;
my lost green fields, the eyes that stare,
the needle pointed pupils
corn-flower blue, the iris black as lunar
landscapes, as bare as southern Spain,
wandering the void of the retina edge.
A dance of dread to watch
a woman whinny in the Portobello Star
her lip drawn back upon her canines,
the blood upon her arm, the two sweet pearls
too sweet by half, each side her mouth,
she used my belt and I could somehow taste
it in myself. Wry, spittled,
intimate; the brand saliva
hawser that betrays like tears,
a viaduct, a stem upon the orifice,
it seemed,
from lip to lip, trailing, trailing
sputum. Those Egyptians knew their teeth

and stood outside a locked-up Sphinx
carrying sandbags empty of songs, at
three o'clock, in the Portobello Road.

The Wicked Messenger

They say he used to send her such
dismembered parts of animals
as frogs' legs – flesh split from flesh –
or spawn in a galvanised bucket,
and that nightly she would take them,
owls' limbs, the backs of alligators,
& crustaceans of the breathless world
& the dinosaurs that sing in trees
while he was waiting for a watch-face
in the early early morning light
as blue as blue as ever was:
they say he sent her shellfish
and dead men in a bottle,
a handful of dice thrown down on the carpet,
match-sticks in a fire-place,
spilt stains upon the shining tiles;
they say he sent her
torn packets and brown paper parcels;
carapaces of minotaurs,
mushrooms in a garden
feathered by the wind;
they say he used to send her
such cold gifts
and bits and pieces of his mind

Jack Walsh

There will be a meeting,
However short, I grant you,
On the early morning staircase
With no surprise
Gorey-wise and shaped like swans
Oh there will be a meeting
On the staircase
Or maybe in Joan Radnor's room
Should I say it
How all the fine young dead come home
To rest and take it easy
True derelicts of norms.
And that will be a meeting
You silver-green and out of face
Long nails
To rip my breast and make me drink,
The grave demands grave cloths
And there will be a cerement
I swear
Too late, sweet heart, I offer forms.

O Bakelite Miz Moon

Jump a hundred times
and then get laid
this is no horror movie
but late at night and I'm afraid
I tried to say I couldn't sleep
a bottle to my mouth
but looking backwards over time
there's no sense of drought
and I believed you when you told me
that all green cheques were green –
greenbacks – slap a dollar
this lady has been seen
in Banks with her machine-gun
holding-up her own
I will salute you and respect you
oh bakelite Miz Moon.
A heartbreak on the telephone
sparks off a certain lapse
a gentle lady in her cradle
an age, a meaning and a breast;
we must have met light-years back
by the evil-winded sea
when you displayed your cuff-links
in your bed of porphyry,
and did you amid the daylight
when the hours had crawled away
& they'd locked you in the close wing
– every swan must have her day –
find it written on the ceiling
as a moustache curling outward
a black and nonsense notion –
did you find my lips too turgid

in the sex scenes in the Motel
where we played the hangman's wedding
with Doctors of Divinities
and nurses at your elbow
while we reckoned hours in ounces
and made it down the highway
& I believed you when you told me
that the road had no horizon
as you smiled beneath your vizor
as you checked your magazine
and you got us to tomorrow
my sweet bakelite Miz Moon.

Ophelia, Sing To Me

There is a cliff beyond my bedroom window,
four floors falling turning over,
there is a door that opens inward
but I have no mirror & so I cannot see
whose face grins over my shoulder ...
a revenant and reject from Cervantes,
formed out of glass & so translucent
though if he be the one I think
there is no surface that could take his print
no casting-light from any planet ...
But I have listened to the serpent
hissing, waiting in the garden,
keeping nightly vigil
in the vineyard and then again in Dublin,
nor can the serpent move on glass
nor could this serpent cast reflection
I'll make a ghost of him as lets me
& walk the battlements of Elsinore ...
(There is a cliff beyond my bedroom window
and the unappeasing dark. Father,
God, forgive us all this thankless task)
Tonight I watch the silver moon through glass
recording still some aspect of this world ...
I'll make a ghost of him as lets me
& walk the battlements of Elsinore:
there is no surface that could take his print –
A strawman on an open road
he walks expectantly before me leaving shoes
and folklore traps and dervish leaves,
he waits in some deserted country lane
against the ditch beneath the dripping winter trees
We'll meet in Styxville, Deathstyx County,
On the Styxville Prohibition Train.

The Hospital Cafeteria

... greetings Mr Diver
I suppose it's no surprise
seeing you here
The liver, he said, collapse?
What kind of death would that be?
Well, said I, (thinking on my feet),
What price range did you have in mind,
Something off the shelf say
Or an exclusive designer all stops out
Little Black Number?
No no no, he said laughing. Neither
Really, but a poor old bugger
Took an hour and a half the other night
And I was wondering ...
far overhead Mr Diver
shakes out another nervous step
on the high wire
The Artist clapped his hands. He said:
There was a noise in his throat
Kind of gruff a strange hoarse noise
He sounded like a cow,
There were two in there with him
A Bible a Nurse and a Doctor –
I looked over the partition –
And they couldn't do anything really.
Nothing that I could see. He was getting on
I suppose, and that was it just looking
And I was wondering
holyroller trembling Mr Diver
jerks a reversible double sommersault
sweating over his coffee cup ...

70

Rockpools

1.
The distance of the glass ordains
the angles between stars and eyes
so looking deep into the mirror pool
she saw light years away
the flickering dog-star and the plough
And now it's little she remembers
her tearstained airmail letter to Paris
where fountains take the place of pools
and drunkenly I sang the Mass
and meant it too with someone else
The substance in the glass ordains
the character of chance or change

2.
The pen in my hand encumbers
both instinct and thought
confuses for a moment craft and numbers
and the white page – wilful as wind
remains the landscape of the albatross
mountainous blank unmarked

But gulls riding on an updraft
make flying look easy
past cliff-ledge and spindrift
ocean and sea-spray
innocent of sepia cuttle-fish ink
unaware of the quills in their wings

3.
In the aspen-leaved morning
he walks and thinks of lakes
lakes caught upon the summits of mountains
lakes green with islands
or blue with hard fish – plantings
cold hard and bare are the woods
in the aspen-leaved morning in winter

Shades of Ranelagh: 1984

As I came in from Drown Lake Mountain
Starved of money and dry to the bone
Where many long years back all burned out
Another exploded sixties myth I was
Caught good & proper on a judge's ruling
And my schooldays wheeled up Ranelagh Road.
As always in discipline I found me walking,
Before and after, all along Vergemount,
Where the Muckross girls drift by like clouds.
Is original sin still alive and well
On the shaded paths of the Dodder?
Does the fashion parade throw a daily shape
To the Bridge and Portobello,
Does everything stop at the Grand Canal
Including the four ten bus to Yuma?
Do the celluloid cowboys up in the Sandford
Still yodel the blues in pure valerian,
Taking tokes and pulling strokes
On the high chaparral of the fire escape
Where Homer nods to Rowdy Yates?
As I sail in from Drown Lake Mountain
On a nineteen forties turf-boat order
I sight my barge on the filled-in harbour
And dance my jigs without embargo,
By the Grand Canal where all things stop
My ballast is weight of Selskar Rock

Houserules

Hoop-la said my working wife
this woman says there were two kinds of amazons
(and she looked at me over her tee ell ess)
the ones who went in for househusbands
and the others ... random copulators
who only hit the ground in spots

Measuring-up to my responsibilities
I called to my wife starting out for work
could you take my head into town today please
have my hair cut and my beard trimmed
for this poetry reading on Thursday
(I was dusting my high-heeled Spanish boots)

Gladly: she threw the talking head
in the back of the car with her lecture notes
her handbag fur coat and galley proofs
tricks of trade and mercantile accoutrements
Otrivine stuffed firmly up my nostrils
to stop catarrh and Hacks for my throat

Leaving me headless and in some straits:
considering the ways of well set-up amazons
as I fumbled helplessly around the garden
playing blind man's buff to a dancing clothesline
stubbing my pegs on air and thinking with envy
of my neighbour and his empire of cabbages

Three Figures In A Pub With Music

And since it has to be a pub scene faute de mieux
take one fat man spread upon a bar stool
talking of Billie Holliday's Strange Fruit
                    Garotted by the slit eyes
on his left he launches into relativity
Einstein he says was only his opinion
and don't ever – lifts glass – degenerate opinion
                    The instruments
I admire the most are the trumpet and the voice
I don't Strange Fruit remember if the blacks were free
he lurches through an instantaneous high C

and slit eyes picks up faultless on the melody
O Mein Papa and Eddie Calvert was magnificent

                    His dexterous friend
the donkey-jacket-over-duck-egg-blue despite
initial difficulty in the depth of field
regains some clarity of tone and brain and pitch
                    (why am I so Black & Blue)
while slit eyes does a private quick-step to the jacks
and disappears the props and stools are switched
on absent friends the orchestra lights up the two
                    with martial music
for chat of history and politics and work and sex
and first name heads of state and drink and revolution
and melting dusty ice fills up the cracks

                    the dying notes
of Tipperary Far Away in Spanish Harlem

Days Of May 1985

In the village street a stained-glass artist
Is trawling the shops for Brunswick Black
On a morning when my head is taken up with light
And light effects on silver halides

Or in Russells on a bleary Wednesday
Clients push in chafing and shooting their cuffs
Signalling pints but "spirits out first please"
Such are the limits of a year's horizons

This week brought Paul Durcan's postcard
With news of Robert Frost and mention of Mt Lafayette
A catalogue of timber in New Hampshire
And yesterday my wife sailed in from Paris

To find me dressed again in campaign summer gear
Which doesn't differ much in truth from winter's
The addition or the stripping of a layer plus decorations
For my regimental Thursdays in the mad house

Being thus torpedoed I must have my story straight
And in my ley-lines find a bill of credence
Pick up on Leeson Street where I was born –
In the Appian Way my bones of childhood mock me

Yet these May mornings toiling to the Nursery
I sense my father's ghost in the wheeling migrant birds
And soon I can accept the electric invitation
Of my amazing son to the breathless world of cherry flowers

Closeup

He is my neighbour yet
he puzzles me – he is a threat up there
guarding the summer shoulder of the hill
perched upon sticks and busy as an insect
                    first time we met
he choked off my tentative *buon giorno*
(and ever since although his wife replies)
                    gruff and locked
in the narrow gauge of his daily
crab-slide from the doorway to the shade
and the waiting car seat set
by the furnace wall beneath the autumn grapes

he is a *bella figura* man of substance

                    his photograph
will find due place
with the others ranked along the cemetery wall
the Bevagnas and the Rossis not in prayer

but as now in slippers and woolen cap he stares
down the ridges of the valley to the road below
a partisan planning an ambush

or putting order on the seasons
he has marshalled them and marked them out with feast days
crippled he is impervious to accident

                    or weather
it is September now and he is out to check
that Polythene is fastened on the wood piles

stirrup pump in hand he stumps the barricades
he is opaque and undefeated

        and why
should I know more about him than this bare account
reckoned against such camouflage
the wind picks up and whispers through the graveyard

        that is all
soon they will be tying down their houses for the winter
the year is done

green lizards dart fearless in the noonday vines
where light itself is sharp and green

Lazarus In Fade Street, Summer 1986

This afternoon in Fade Street in the sun
all these ancient gestures
and all those flickering acid lights
they ... *don't touch me any more*
come home from harvesting the years
I have gathered in my tribe and wives
and tied the haggard door

thinks Lazarus in Fade Street in surprise

come home at last to roost
like a retired sea captain
without support or sycophants
I am watching how the operators work
taking a bearing in my own backyard
on the shifting of brick and emphasis
the architecture of the New Ireland
and noticing the architects by name

Oh Alice Glenn
Lady of Astronomical Compassion
Pray for us now and in Leinster House Amen

and I feel I was more cherished underground:

consistent in my generation
spent maybe twenty years entombed
just looking out and listening to the rain
achieving wisdom and no position
a nineteen sixties solipsist –
thus I reserve my own defence –

filling in the cracks in time until
the door swung open and I shook myself awake
rolled off my bed of snakes
and travelled home like a fault to roost
a cherished child of the State
my pockets full of unsigned cheques
faded unpresented dreams
manifests of phantom ships
dry salt I gathered off Cape Horn
dry salt for wounds the curing of:

no need for gothic narrative thinks Lazarus

Ronald Reagan is made a Doctor of Laws
pray for us now in Leinster House

something is happening here

Peter Barry is selective in his strictures
I listened hard but heard
no echoes of outrage when Tripoli was bombed

and I don't know what it is
do you Mr. Bones?

And yes – who speaks for me in this
coming up out of the ground
a fading Signorelli figure strayed from Orvieto
making my way home from Waldo's Wood?
I feel threatened in this referendum
by the aggressive razzmatazz of family men
I have a family but I cannot share
the appalling certainty of Padraig Flynn:

who conjures *me* in Fade Street?

Lazarus without an audience
emerging into daylight stumbles in the dust
steadies himself by the Castle Market
consults his chart and makes for home
the high road home from Cesena
veteran of hospital and lock-up
here's where we part company perhaps
finding another way through the waste lots
turning off at the fireworks factory

and singing: *flat road yellow moon*
coming home at night through fields of sunflowers

Stopping The Lights, Ranelagh 1986

1.
Two hands to the bottle of Wincarnis
this timeless gent his cap turned back to front
arranges himself in the delta of downtown Ranelagh
and sits on the public bench first
carefully hitching his trousers at the knee
preserving the delicate break over the instep
advised by Bertie Wooster's Jeeves
he hefts the bottle up and sucking deep
with one eye shut he draws a bead

Secure in his well constructed tree top hide
Lord Greystokes fixes on the jungle
in between the changing of the traffic lights
like drops of blood the amber jewels of his rood
accurately lights a cigarette
The lion – he mouths – *The lion sleeps tonight*
the traffic beacons change
controlled and manageable their peacock march
from green to red and red to green
Ring out wild bells: he settles back

A businesslike nun swims into frame
intervenes in a pale cold car behold
and disengaging gear
reflects a while in Gordon's hardware shop
the glass of her aquarium is hung
with buses plastic basins toasters
electric kettles lengths of timber super-glue
bronze fire-dogs brooms and Bilton dinner sets
here on the veldt

she brings a missionary whisper
the folded mysteries of convent breakfasts
white linen and starched altar cloths
white cattle birds half glimpsed in Africa
lights flash cars slip into gear slide off

And the delta has become my launching pad
my swampland Florida
junkyard of burnt-out rocket systems
where all that thrust falls back to earth
to rust in secret in the Corporation Park
my blue eyed son is friend to man
and guides me through the shadowy tangled paths
where alligators twine and lurk
and I learn to recognise my lunar neighbours
among mysterious constellations

2.
It takes some time to make an epic
or see things for the epic that they are
an eighteenth century balloonist
when Mars was in the Sun set out for Wales from here
trailing sparks ascended through the clouds
and sank to earth near Howth
while dancing masters in the Pleasure Gardens
played musical glasses in the undergrowth
they have used the story to rename a pub
to make a Richard Crosbie of the Chariot

And we too
have come through dangers and we call
to the MC on the console *stop the lights*
here at the wrong end of the telescope
my one concern is holding down the present

Sunday mornings on the Great South Wall are real
and hand in hand with Niall
it is enough
when we are astral travellers and our astral turf
the cut blocks that interlock upon each other
and we are inaccessible and far off dots
on the Half Moon road to the lighthouse
safe from the law alive and well
in the wind on the Great South Wall

1987 – 1994

Words From A One-Way Ticket

I came abreast of my forty-sixth year Captain
since last I saw you –
nine hours out of Paris on the Napoli Express
six of us at five-twenty-five AM
stretched out in our couchette
on the wings of triplanes
wrapped in disposable fabrics
we are hot cryonics in a honeycomb
lifting up on the occasional elbow
to angle for the dawn –
and missing it at Torino Porta Nuova
the cormorants bobbed awake at Genova
put on their daytime faces for La Spezia
where I fell down a marble staircase once –
But no stopping this time Captain
we will go beneath the hills past Pisa
in Florence maybe have a cup of coffee
and make my through connection for Teróntola

Always hopeful of the great adventure
I listen to their heartbeats and survey the years
noting how we submerge like submarines
to surface maybe a decade later
when we are travelling down some Autostrada
and the rhythm sets a train of thought in motion
until late in the hazy afternoon
poised and quick on some foreign cross-roads
or striding some railway platform
you meet yourself and learn that you are someone else
that all these years you have been someone else –
a civil servant in Salamanca

with a wife and child and mistress –
who sits too long over drinks in the evening
in some shadowed sandstone square playing dice
But while he survives I am moving into
another kind of bandit country
to learn what happens after forty-five:

The trees were bare when we arrived
it was thundery and cold
the kind of weather you imagine did for Shelley
and we burned the off-cut logs from the mill
but now on this last day of April
I can see clear across the Plain of Umbria
and the clusters of houses dotted on the hill-tops
bear Aristotelian witness
to the sympathy of stone –
no colour here seems out of place
where everything that is has rein to riot –
There is order in the frenzy of the light
all along the slopes beneath this terrace
I see the ranked descent of vines and olives
Figures of Etruscan Geometry:

And Captain – when I consider it
what else could I have done but travel on?
Is that not all there is?
Yet for the moment now I take a pause
naked on this Italian roof
under Monte Subasio to make an act of faith
drinking black tobacco in the sun

Street Scenes: February 17th 1987

1.
A large backside camouflaged in a telephone kiosk
a self-help group flashes by in an Ambulance
                                        & Roisín
eating sticky buns in the front seat of a car
cradling a sink-unit

2.
Driving past the Jesuits at night
I hear the ghosts of women in the Milltown Flats

3.
Cold bright northern weather
parents are getting frisky at the school gates
Election posters have bloomed around the lamp-posts

4.
All this is Yuppy Country
says the PD activist:
God doesn't play dice and McDowell gets in

5.
But at the corner of Aston Place and Bedford Lane
I read:
        Yobbo & Kosh
        Auds & Tommo
        Lorna & Martin
        Lisa & Stud
in white paint more permanent than print

The Egyptian Singer

That's all very well I said
to the painted angel on the festoon blind
that's all very well but
there's no love here no sensual heat
or none that I can make out
She threw her head back
clicked her fingers – What?
No love here? Don't be ridiculous –
she paused – on the other hand
it depends on what you want I suppose

There is a man outside my window
lithe as a cat
picking magic mushrooms
walking like a cat on the wet grass
caught up in his concentration
I have been watching him for hours
and for some time I thought he was picking worms
it is all so distant
picking worms or mushrooms
it depends on what you want I suppose

That Egyptian singer in the background
I listened to her when I was drunk
night after night with my hair matted
falling down the stairs
or staggering up to bed
and now I sit here
in a cone of hard white light
while she sings of love and sex and loneliness
it depends on what you want I suppose

Fellow Passengers

Words come falling
from this silhouette
coiled up tight
with his back to the light
fragments of words –
twitching and dangerous

I see him blunted
reader of the Sun
bringing our boys back home
tatooed with blood and printed
on his left hand MICK
jerking in the undergrowth
deranged and dangerous

Some unequal force
smashed a bottle
in his skull at birth –
he reaches out
to stab his fingers in my face:
Can I have a
have a light then? Hey?

Bit of all
Bit of all right then?
Sits down his fingers
beating on the table top
takes up his friend and quest again:
The Jewman in James' Street
you know the poofter him

In and out job – quick
no hanging about
know what I mean? Are you on?
The beast is loose
persuasive now
he drops his eyes
his claws and tongue protrude

Him on the hill
he wheedles
him on the hill is King
is King – you know what I mean?
He wets his lips and whispers
It was after –

I was there my son
and it was after –
after sweet michelle
he done her in

After The Slane Concert – Bastille Day 1987

The dark girl drinking cider in the bar
smiles speaking of her knife
my ears prick at the hint of violence
with thoughts of a dark street in Paris
almost thirty years ago
stoned high and fighting with a one-eyed Arab
above that Metro shelter
the quick flash of violence and sex
and short knives stabbing across the street

He was pissing sideways says the girl
like he wasn't aiming straight
and ... and here her voice drops out of sight
her hair mingles with her neighbour's
like curtains falling across the street
I think of Borges' Argentinians
dying in limelight under street lamps
it is all so casual so promiscuous
so soft these lethal beautiful parishioners

And was it really just like this –
an inner city pub where careless Fates
blast on cider and cigarettes
so sure footed and so self-contained
so dangerous
the smile that seems as innocent of violence
as the knife-blade in its hidden place
and one maimed look is all it needs
to make us human
reading in the morning ash for messages of love

Seconds Out

After Humpty Dumpty fell apart
they said they would reconstitute him
in the Tat factory
iron out the folds in his carapace
rebuild him with sellotape and cowgum
three square meals a day
and some confrontation therapy

It would be hard they said
a stiff course for an egg
– an egg who suspected he'd be better off
robbing mail trains
or turning tricks on the canal bank –
a stiff course for an egg
but they would make a man of him

As in the end they did
a man of weights and measures
stripping five thousand crocus flowers
to procure an ounce of saffron:
in Cambodia there is no more gamboge yellow
and at the speed of light
sons are older than their space-men fathers

In The Ranelagh Gardens: Easter Saturday 1988

Easter falls early this year
at the end of a mild winter –
tomorrow the sun will dance on the ceiling
at midnight on Thursday by the sea I heard
Summer rustling in the palms

Listen said the voice
for years I have been fighting my way up out of this
climbing out of this black hole
pushing past the bog oak
and this black weight that hugs my rib cage

On a street corner in Rome my brother-in-law
the Guardian of Paradise reflects
Arabian gentleman in camel hair
how can I have grown so old he says
staring into his daughter's camera lens

I thought of him again last night
and looked for design in our ad hoc lives
breathing cool air from the surface of the pond
remembering I must not be in competition
not even with myself

Listen said the voice
for years I have been in the shallows of this lake
a creature of the reeds
hunting under drowned and folded leaves
with the water beetles

Angelica Saved By Ruggiero

This girl I recognise her
from the filleting room at the back of Keegan's
dismembering North Sea haddock saithe and spur-dog
now at nine o'clock in the morning
I watch her striding through the dry-ice air
red hair the colour of insides of sea-urchins
herself like an underwater creature
she flits and darts through the morning traffic
wrapped around in her red and white stripes
to the shade and shell of her souk

I caught her in a net and brought her home one night
as befits me a convicted anarchist
who himself keeps a roadside stall in Tripoli
not far from the Azizia barracks
a thousand miles east of the Rue Bab Rob
one month's journey through the territory of ostriches
a two month journey travelling by ostrich
subsisting only on their chalky eggs

I seized her like a myth and brought her home
to this courtyard market and charnel shambles
my carpeted rooms up under the roof
sat her on the floor and to protect her from the night
wrapped her in a kefia from Damascus
gave her a gold-work kaftan and slippers for her feet
filled glasses of mahia from Marrakesh
served mejoun and mint tea on an inlay table
and coffee taken from the heat three times
thick black coffee from Cairo

And up beneath the slippery roof
we skewered fish kebabs and prawns for a feast
clams caught that morning in Essaouria
while we gazed out through the windows at the sky
past Rats' Castle and the old men's home
beyond the Burlington to the mouth of the river
suspended in the silver nitrate moon
and the minarets of the Pigeon House
until I saw her deep-sea eyes cloud up

This happens in mid-sentence
with our fingers on the page we lose our place
delaying we were caught between the tides
while the foreshore lengthened all around
into a dim anonymous suburban pub
with the elements and furniture of sea-wrack
rising up from the floor to claim us
ash-trays and razor-shells a palm-court pianist
and in the corner hung with sea-weed
a supermarket trolley rusting in the sand

The level sands stretched out and that was it
new myths spring up beneath each step we take
always another fact or proposition missed
and just for a moment we almost touched
though she knows nothing of it now in cold December
dancing out of the Ingres painting
and making her way down the morning street
she pauses in mid-stride then looks away
freed from that scenario of chain and rock
Andromeda – this girl – I recognise her

Man On The Doorstep

after the summary killings by the SAS in Gibraltar 1988

He knocks on my door at night
the howling storm made visible
raves at me like conscience
come out he says come out
come out and see the holes in the road
the holes in the road in the rain
it is all falling down around us
holes full of water for children to fall in
and he is right –
five minutes is all it would take
take five to walk to the bottom of the hill
to see these childrens' graves in the rain

But I can't go out
because I am minding a real live child
I am father to a child
who eats and sleeps and goes to school
flies kites and brings me paintings
and keeps his margins to the edge of the page
or as near as he can at five and a half
who is not for the moment homeless
and depends on me to keep the night outside

Tá Bran ar scoil
Tá Mici ag gáire Tá Lulu ag gol

No you can't come out says the man
but you can go to bloody Umbria –
and what are you going to do about this

Fascist descent into Anarchism?
What are the artists of Ireland doing?

Safeguard your reputation

I was here this morning in this very place
in this very place today – and
he digs his heel into the crumbling pavement –
and I said to an Indian doctor
an Indian doctor from the College of Surgeons
how can people live in this
in this city falling apart
seeing this same shit day after day and every day
head shaking like John O Gaunt
this same shit and nothing else
enough said said the doctor –

Do you realise
that in the European Parliament
the whole of Europe is laughing at us?
The Germans are laughing at us
the Italians the French
the Greeks and Spaniards are laughing
laughing into their translation machines
laughing like drains
like the rain falling on Dublin they laugh
and the British shoot us

He moves away into the night –
Safeguard your reputation with Cess-Clean
says the advertisement on national radio

Street Scenes: The Perpetual Laundrette

In the café window seat
looming in leather jacket
buckskins and bodywave
he sits up and says
it's the stupidest thing in the world you know
to point a gun at someone –
to point a gun at someone he nods
and not pull the trigger

Beside him enthuses
a wide-eyed breathless girl
oh it is oh it is oh it is
and just like that
they have it all worked out
here by the Perpetual Laundrette

And I am wondering
where I might find clean clothes –
really clean clothes
that smell of mountain flowers
carded and separated fibres
lighter than journeys in sun and snow –
not stiff with age and guilt
and battered train trips
from Dublin to London London to Dublin
coloured by memories of Collis Browne
and weariness
and the killing fields at Crewe

A proud male transient
        he stamps the plastic
spoons and knives into the floor –

Why do you live in a country
where it rains all the time?
And bitch about it?
It seldom drops past seventy in Mexico
and you can live on a dollar a day –
maybe more if you smoke cigarettes

From the corner:
Why do Foreigners come over here?

Beneath the table out of sight
of their companions
she lays her hand upon his thigh
little bird
it rivets me

Outlined against the inside of the window
with Merry Xmas and Christmas trees reversed
she extends a finger
and he moves upon it mouthing like a fish
licks her hand and sucks her cuticle

Gathering my coat about me
I rise to leave
thinking of a summer in Berkshire
of sometimes sleeping rough
and on the morning after
watching a breathless wide-eyed girl
in a field drink Johnnie Walker

The Bella Figura, Ranelagh

Of a sudden in the afternoon
I found him
lurking motionless and purposeful
breath suspended
in the shade in my long front garden
a man from the pub
who is all mankind or was
Is he not my neighbour like the rest
even those who persecute and …

It is not clear what he is at
red faced and caught off guard
he pretends to be staring at the wall
then strikes out accusingly
angrily – By God he says
By God but you've made a great recovery –
Do you know that?
I remember when no one could talk to you

That is enough now –
I shall die of that
Said Ferdia

Little Hound –
In one of these houses another neighbour
an elderly woman
broke her hip last week
and treated the break with Wintergreen
treated the break for days with Wintergreen
In our arms we carried her
from bed to threshold

by the River Swan
on the riverbank we laid her down
in the shelter of chariot wheels

Too well tempered by the ghosts
and vampires who walk up and down my stairs
clothed in memories of MIMS Directory
I am weary of ignorance
and still locked up –
still watching the prison weather cock
weary of ignorance
and tired of visitations

What incarnations in the garden
surprise – resentment
or reverberation of skulls beneath the hearthstone
mislead you to believe
that we are talking
that we have anything to say
that you are talking to me now?

Long Day Short Night She Dances

1.
Drums coalesce the beat steps up
and she dances out eyes down makeshift
she slides across the sandy floor
arms lifted like a child
little more than a child she is
the household's daughter
an endangered balancing act
juggler in the family group
Soho whiskies and her mother's brandies
reflect acryllically about her steps
shanghaied and hijacked by a myth
the legend of her father
she is too old now for the show – too old
to be tossed around like Buster Keaton
too young to be sawn in half like this –
a black ball rolls across the floor
as we remember it
she had been dancing thus for years

2.
On cue tonight the band strikes up
the floating platform band
his mouth a husk the singer struts
with bulging microphone in hand
he tries for geographical escapes

Take me down to the Shining City
the industrial chimneys and the lots
life is short and your lips are soft
take me down by the shore tonight
take me down by the river steps

on the seaward side of the railway tracks
take me out to Buenos Aires

the sea is glutinous and quiet
with an orange moon above the mountains
night stops at the Hill of Howth
and fire-ships in the bay light up
the shrouded figures here
the lay-by flash of thigh and breast
these timeless isolated
lovers of the dark

3.
It is afternoon the town is shut
I am here in the sun in an open boat
holding a small black owl in my hand
I am a child
a woman leaning toward me leaning forward
ringed fingers glinting on the oars
backwards and forwards back and forth
giving me birth or swallowing me up
sculls us to an island
we are newly eloped from her mother's house
sailing across the bay to freedom
a back-parlour bar up against the cliff
filled with tackle and tack
the smell of leather and sherry wine
and sun and skin and innocence:
before the boat can reach the slip
the black owl drops from my hand
and falls to the swimmers far beneath
so many swimmers
so many countless pilot fish

21-6-1989

Sharing Houseroom

At night you can see around the corner
in the mirror in the corridor
depths deeper than the lake
at the end of that tubular perspective
another hallway and a door
upon another landscape
a door with spring-action iron bolts
above the ascendant steps
the trim box-wood
and the elusive carriageway beneath –
So much for the Set:

On call
throughout the afternoon we wait
for mirror-spots to point our marks
and give us room to move –
the director sits behind a curtain
his pockets full of stones
with which to pelt the audience
– if indeed we have an audience –
playing Argentinian dance-music
and the air is sweet
with tobacco smoke and dust

The language will be silent
the language to be used
when finally he calls on us for action
language of an age
when invitations were spontaneous
the widening of the iris
sweat on the lip

quickening of body-heat
erectile hairs
swift familiar acrid scents
and in that invented place of taste and touch
there will be urgencies
and urgency will bring it off

In the meantime the house is ours
more or less –
full of scene-shifters and birds of passage
lighting-men and an undertaker
driving nails in the attic

And in the meantime carefully
alone behind our several doors
like absent friends we rehearse ourselves
plot fantasies
interpret our edgy symptoms
eat – sleep
parcel up sheets for the laundry
listening always for sounds of contact
footsteps in the room above
the creaking riser on the stairs
a cough or sob in the corridor
and waiting always always straining
for that quick catch of breath

Death In Venice: Panicale, August 1989

You opened a gate in a field
for the hanged man to shamble out
after years of fencing –
and I thank you for the summons
will you dress me for the part?
What cover should I wear
to go back to Venice for the day
al fresco on the Lido
in the Strawberry Beds in the open air –
long beige woolen scarf
battered felt hat?
Smart tie and handkerchief
jewellery and scents –
von Aschenbach himself descending
the stairs to meet the Press?

It is important –
some time today in the afternoon
we play the death scene
maybe naked
or maybe you will wear a long Edwardian dress
Victorian elastic-sided boots
and the light of course will be perfect
under your wide-brimmed hat –
thus far it is a fantasy
flesh and blood but still a fantasy –
we are in a cornfield
alone together in the full scirocco
put here by the make-up man
with ice and wine
and water to keep down the dust

It is a fantasy
in a field we have not entered yet
some nameless lot past Chapelizod
I see you standing waving
turning from the waist up
one hand resting on your hip
beckoning and pointing
pointing to a Summer in Provence
with the Îles d'Hyères on the horizon
and we are both nineteen again
working on the vendange
penniless and truly burnt
working our way to the head of the field
and the water and wine and blocks of ice
in the shade in a wooden box

It is later now and tense
in this imaginary garden –
the strawberry vendor has been
with his basket of dead-ripe fruit
there is a cloud along the Lido and the river
children's voices in the cornfield
and women calling them back
Tadziu – the sound hangs in the trees
Tadziu Tadziu – the woman with the pearls –
but we play out the fantasy
streaked with sweat and dust
diving coming up for air
recording each others' imprint
until night
and the light we know will be perfect

The Country Of Blood-Red Flowers

Looking out the window
six hours since I heard the Angelus
and there is no heavenly music
in the air above the house

Waiting for the dancer
to arrive across the fields tonight
with bag and bandages – a black
silk blindfold for my eyes

The window is unbarred
for locked cells may not be opened
where we find ourselves
in the country of blood-red flowers

Red flowers that bloom
at random in the chambers of the brain
along the blood
and lock into the mind and heart

She waits and she is right
little coelacanth – serpent brother
out there in the forest undergrowth
I hear her hesitate

Looking for patterns
she reformulates her steps –
again to the light of our lost rooms
love brings its own contagion

The Mirror-fish

Too much alone
I am uneasy here –
this silver light selects
lights random images

One day in Vezelay
approaching through the fields
my head dizzy
it was hard to breathe
under the weight of the great stone roof
red tumbrils of Côte du Rhone –
at the cut stone foot
of that cascading cliff of stone
a sick bat trapped
at the base of a column
in a shaft of sunlight
crawled nakedly for shade
mouth open
head thrown back
small teeth small rictus lips

Abandon had I known it
in a nearby house
a woman I had lived with
was making love
behind an eighteenth century façade
in an eighteenth century bed
looking down upon the orchard
making love in French

Years after in my turn
after the reunification of Italy
I came to myself in an empty bed
with all that world
that Ancien Regime
gone over to the enemy
to find the bat returned
a wistful outstretched messenger
a hanging crucifix
small trapped childish face
hunched up – stapled by the sun
to the mosquito blind

Hanging drunk
hanging like a tipsy sailor
or a passenger in panic
on a ship going down
hanging in the rigging
head thrown back and to the side
transfixed –
Santa Maria della Vittoria
I knew a woman once in Vezelay
with that same rictus of the lips

The moon is up
and in this solitude and nightmare
nothing is resolved –
moving unseen
I am a tarpon fish
the large mirror of these scales
reflects the ocean
the inner deeps
this sheet of water here beneath the moon –
this is not translucence

Time And The Ice-fish

This is it now the lighthouse
any further we can not
than the sea-wall's end
like the others we must drop back

This week-end – in a day or less
they are turning the clocks back
and we will hear the cogs mesh
and the minutes begin to tick

Because there is no respite
from the knowledge in the blood
this is a fearful country this
bleak landscape of the ice-fish

Miz Moon

Just one time more Miz Moon
here by the lakeside waiting for the dark
testing out these inland moorings
milestones and mornings in fading rooms –
do you remember the rooms Moon?
The smell of rooms?

Dust after rain in Marrakesh
sweet smell
cummin and coriander blowing on the wind
cedar and cream and almonds
jus d'amandes
okra rosemary petrol-fumes and kif

Running before the wind Moon
every day down to this
museum of furniture and memories and rooms
all to be vacated before noon
I hook onto phrases pictures scents –
do you remember the Delfin Verde?

Or white mornings up in Azrou
temporary cool in the Rif
and the smell of cool crisp flowers in the Atlas –
our tiled hotel in Ouarzazate
a nestling cruciform scorpion
asleep under the arch of my boot

Patterns of grace notes –
the bat's wing stretched is a dusty leaf
there is no one now beneath the willow
but blue and vacant glaze

and on the stairs at night I smile for the camera
this time turned by a ghost

Looking down now like Peter Quint
I see two figures in a boat traverse the lake
laughter after movement
till distance takes them in among the trees
we inhabit rooms of pictures Moon
ceramic pictures: painted plates

    *

Who is this Moon you ask
who is Miz Moon?
Like a trumpet blast in Cordoba
Moon in the morning throws the shutters open
with a Chinese finger on your pulse
sensuous Moon is focused

Moon is wild garlic
after forty years of determined self-destruction
of giving the bump and grind to time
she has time now only for the jugular
free of politesse or politics
urgent Moon is infamous

Infamous Moon
making a monstrous lizard of the road
screwed everyone she met until
the alkali desert south of Albacete
cool Moon riding – on a crate
of Carlsberg Special and an ounce of dope

Robbed banks
became a figure on surveillance tape
took a Diploma in History –
affected a Nurse's uniform
to run Crimi's Venereal Clinic in Naples
until Doctor Crimi turned her out for drink

Went to pieces in Tortosa
from the bodyweight of alcohol and Crimi's pills
jumped from a balcony
and holding six broken ribs in place
retracing her shambling steps
drove non-stop from Barcelona to Le Havre

Missed the boat
and sank without trace –
Her progress halted she is all of this
and yet which one is Moon?
I hear party sounds from Sunset Boulevard
and Von Stroheim in the garden breaking ice

                    *

Fearful of rejection
I am too quick to put the blame on Moon
her indecision and her machinations
those fantastic ill timed assignations
I wonder if she ever could speak straight
until I remember Moon herself is hurt

No better suited for rejection
she has seen too many years in bars
too many afternoons in bed
fighting with hangovers and sleeping sickness

she understands too well
that stump of flesh we carry round

And what have I in turn to bring to Moon
here and now domestic me
that I should take her sometime lover's place
keeping my hot eyes off her daughter
every old man jack of me?
He gave her a child and was good about the house

All day today I walked the house
and the outhouse buildings and the forest path
keeping my side of the tryst
keeping myself for Moon at last
no Moon and the double cross cuts deep
etched in my window by the dawn

And at this point Miz Moon herself
the real Miz Moon
steps from the door to the hall porter's desk
sound of the oud and Oum Khalsoum
signs her name with a curlew feather
oval-eyed innuendo Moon

Now Moon and I in our separate corners
are much like any other couple
I haul the luggage up
she pauses on the stairs to order breakfast
we kick the fading fire awake
and sleep untroubled by fidelities

*

With Moon in the Botanic Gardens
I stepped into a Chinese print
of figures hidden in among the leaves
saffron horsemen on a hill
a woman dancing with a fan
in pools of white behind the evergreens

By the oriental stream in Finglas
Moon rested for a time
beneath a variation of the willow
Moon spoke of Highland flowers
what I missed most up there she said
was the simple sound of birds

There was no birdsong on the crags
when Moon went walking on the Mongol border
athletic Moon on tour
climbed over tor and fell and scar
horned goat-Moon
kneeling at every crescent station

Restless Moon slips under glass
strolls drily through the beds of cacti
spread at her feet like kidney beans
thinks of Arizona and her travels in Peru
lakes and floating islands
and dipping stone-birds on the sea

In the moist air of the hothouse
tropical Moon at last alone
lay down among the roots of bamboos
listened to water dripping from the roof
sloughed off memories and skins
all through the humid afternoon

Moon dined with serpents
satyrs and hyenas coupled in the ferns
supported by a plinth of polished stone
Moon surveys the circus unamazed
disdainfully – a maja Moon
Olympian hand in place Miz Moon reclines

*

Heigh-ho says Moon and what do I want
running away from home like this
taking refuge in the lake –
tangled up in images
turn turn to the wind and the rain
would they leave me be when the job is done?

Creaking down the stairs at night
with a bag of celibate laundry
she feels this is no way to spend a life
turning herself into fantasy
a grown person should be more urgent
more troubled by realities

Understanding the market –
take a course in assertiveness
build mushroom cities and marinas
read and re-read the operators' handbook
and the cost-analysis of friendship
learn to push herself as product

Not turn her head into a voodoo hall
a Grand Guignol burlesque
smoking and going for healthy walks and smoking more
burning forty cigarettes a day

lying awake with pains in the chest
examining herself three times daily

And going outside to spit in private –
dear God says Moon
I have left my two precious lungs in shreds
all over this ornamental garden
I think I shall not be let out –
this white horse goes nowhere

Suddenly swaybacked with desire
Moon closed her eyes and shook her head
borrowed a bag and took time off
booked in for the nearest sea-port town
and slept all night by the harbour wall
with a heigh-ho the wind and the rain

      *

One afternoon in sunlight Moon
lying on a hillside
as she thought safe among the plantings
saplings rising all around her
watched a stain of purple spreading on her arm
what fresh hell is this said Moon

No *mort phthisique* for Moon
despite what might be waiting in the script
she did not intend to start upon a slow decline
or some day sit silently at table
a superannuated Mafiosa
shrouded against the light

Child of her generation
Moon would always be so blonde on blonde
death if it came for her would come
quick on a summer afternoon
when she was all sex and flesh and fruit
crushed ice and music

Time and genes decided else
and the wild rose grew back upon the stock
fire flashed along the hillside
Moon stared at the purple mark
the purple hair that sprouted from her breast
lake and sky flared suddenly and fierce

Sickened by light
Moon hid away in darkened rooms
watching the shadows of cats through windows
she walked the stone-flagged passages at night
noting the smell of age in the sheets
in a world of mirrors and books

Diehard Moon porphyric self-contained
she moved through all the phases of derangement
dressed in purple by appointment
turned the night to day and dreamed
of far-flung campfires and the glint
of red tinged fluorescent teeth

*

It was not an Aztec dream Moon
you put me in a matriarchal frieze
of women moving as planets move
across cold desert nights –

this woman's eyes devour this man
he stares down at himself in bloom

But a shadow has intruded
some tension grafted on the lovers here
hooked in position
allowed no momentary gesture of desire
I hear a rumour of resentment
reptilian politics

I look again at the Mexican colours
and think of Frida Kahlo –
here in the country of Madre de Dios
we learn our remorse from the waist down
if I use Moon she uses me
what else is there but leaning in to it

And leaning in without regret
the rest is a confusion
of maps and schemes and talk of soixante-huit
and whose design is this –
who marked out this frieze?
Is everyone reptilian in the end?

Hush child said Moon that will do you now
you have said your piece move on
we part again with no regrets
although in truth it has been hard enough
hard enough and I am hollowed out
weary as a stone

Today I watched a bird in flight
above the lake fall faultlessly
stall and fall wheel dip for bait

flying back upon the lake to retrace its path
dropping without regret
fly and stall falter fall and touch

fly stall falter fall and touch

Tavernelle Di Panicale

I woke in panic in the heat
floating through the middle of the night
over the furnace of the pizzeria
not daring to turn on the light
for fear of bringing the mosquitoes in
or waking my son from sleep –

Christ that I could disentangle
just one dimension before the day comes back
working like that Gaelic bard in the womb of the boat
putting the bones of his poem in place –
Captain I am sleeping here below
below decks in the worm bitten rafters

I am putting memories in place
and calling-in on disused expertise –
the eel-net in the shed calls up but cannot save
energies spilled out on sand –
like the lost music of the Horn Concertos
worthless as a fico secco

Dazed and isolated in the garden –
like this new fig-tree planted yesterday
a touch of acid green not much taller than my son
already fixing in the ritual stones
roots sunk in sand to keep them cool –
the day moves on and I am come adrift

To come to in Tavernelle –
we have made a shift to put our house in order
buying beds and hoisting home a fridge
putting a new hose on the butane cooker
having the water analysed
replacing broken windows

All these are basics and still I am adrift –
imprisoned in the evening shade
marked by time and that Sicilian cut
sometimes I feel the sun has failed me
squeezing out the years like juice
without even the choice of maize or sunflowers

We carry on because there is no choice
stung by times to anger and resentment but
without intercession still making a fist of it –
plastering the cracks with functional stucco
hacking at the same impenetrable thorns
hammering at the same blank pages

SCORPIONS

I built a castello of stones and mud
and great baulks of seasoned timber
with oak doors in the walls
and then I whitewashed the walls on the inside
put a fire-back and pots in the fire-place
a new-forged crane and hooks and chain
and in preparation for the siege ahead
I laid in logs and charcoal
onions and oil and garlic
and sides of bacon hanging from the beams

and then I sat back and waited
this whole peninsula was waiting
and I was European and waiting for the Barbarians

That German tonight in Castiglione del Lago
drunk lifted up a woman's dress
his companion night-jars screeching in the dark
pesca di mare pesca di mare
laughing their way up the cobbled street
pesca di mare – pesche di mare
her curved gold abdomen a peach?
And in Panicale yesterday another
a madman torched himself and teenage son
we heard the ambulance climb screaming up the hill
the Corriere dell' Umbria in hot pursuit
and I thought of WeeGee
WeeGee flashing through the New York night
shadowing death for the Saturday Post
and I was European and waiting for the Barbarians

And in the end like dreams they came
black scorpions came down my walls to join me
finding recognition in the whites of my eyes
soot creatures from before my childhood
from that rain-streaked chimney space
black scorpions came down my white-wash walls
and I know the limits of this farm-house hearth
what people occupied this place
my grandmother's bedroom stretching away
away from the house and the hill and the furze
my dead uncles standing like frozen horses
and the beasts that stamp and knock beneath
and I am European and waiting for the Barbarians

SUNFLOWERS

There was a moment I could have caught there
this afternoon on my steps
loose in the sunlight
seen fit to die here
looking down the hazy road toward Tavernelle
and the insects fluttering their day away
above my dusty sunflowers

There was a moment there I almost caught
when I recognised my father in myself
not the young man in photographs
foot on chair in revolutionary stance
but as I see him now
looking at me from the mirror
as I joke with my son about the motorcycle gobdaws
in the fields nearby
churning the red earth up

As I think we might have joked
reporting on the walkie-talkie
about the number of frogs in the irrigation ditch
since the coming of the water-snake
and gone for walks on the hill above the house
or dived for coins in the public pool
travelling together through the language
hand in hand
had we made it to Le Cigne
as we made it to the Shelly Banks

Age and drink dimmed that for us
still there was a moment there
I almost had us in a frame together

cycling through sunflowers down the Liffey Quays
that time you from the crowd
played stand-in for a missing goalie
in the Phoenix Park
forty years ago –
or dying for Ireland on the stage in Dublin
or checking your football pools in Sandymount
hopefully
on Sundays before the pubs opened
or hunting amethysts above Keem Bay for therapy

I remember this
middle-aged on these Italian steps
and understand the downturn of your mouth
under siege and quizzical
echoed in my own
wondering how in the end we got here

Niall plays in the sunny yard below
I bequeath him summer and these sunflowers

Les Côtes Du Tennessee

The colours you will walk in little son
these countries that are yours were mine
were magical and strange such contradictions
the space bat angel spread its wings
and came down burning from the sun
are magical and strange and dangerous
and oh the world is full of crooks and heroes
beware the cargo when your ship comes in
the autumn serpent in the stubble field
those patient spiders in our dusty rooms
have registered and taken note
and hold us in their thousand eyes

Forty-one years later the tune still plays
through this April afternoon my birthday.
in the skies above the Lost River Ranch
Highway 76 and the Mississippi delta
Les Cotes du Tennessee and *Beausoleil*
the space bat dragon loops and sings
make me an angel that flies from Montgomery
send me a poster of an old rodeo
just give me one thing that I can hold on to
and the world is full of crooks and heroes –
I have been listening since East Liberty
since West Palm Beach and since the dawn

Vrai Citoyen du Monde like Thomas Paine
of all the dawns alone or shared in empty rooms
or standing by a ship's rail watching
this self-same Mississippi sun come up
down East of Wexford and the Tuskar Rock

in flight from time and circumstance – at
thirty thousand feet above pretence we start
to drop for Arkansas and South Missouri
new rooms new names new answers friends
as the space bat angel dragon sings
in a world made right for crooks and heroes
that if defeated we fly down in flames

Station Platform: Sandymount

for Pat Boran

At 48 stoop-shouldered come to rest
and grief I say that's it enough
I quit on grief in action and on all of it
disentangled from the truth
such fantasies need time and life
and too much time and life of late –
I'll quit this city and these burning shapes
of smuts and ashes on the wind
smoking and smouldering those neon lights
the snipers under greasy eaves
birds of prey on the bedroom wall
and love in caves beneath the streets

I will find out where this river goes
before it meets the sea – and to deserve
all proffered friendship and affection
I'll salute old friends lost friends
old afternoons from all of twenty years ago
unfold a half-forgotten yellow map
to walk Borodino a while unharmed –
the lock gate opens on the Marne canal
and slow green water spills out over
all the afternoon in Moncourt – Niall and I
are walking side by side this dry July
following the international barges

To see what happens what occurs
behind the trees and round the bend – we come
upon my father skimming stones

these ten years dead and skimming stones
my sabbath father on the shore
alone and dark at Sandymount
by the railway track and the cold sea-baths
come back a black-eyed exorcist
waiting silent where the river goes
before it meets the sea
before we parted company – Can you recall
alive refashion this his black eyes ask?

Look Dad Look – says Niall this afternoon
in Moncourt and cocks a whiplash arm –
This is how your father skimmed a stone

The Banks Of The Danube: The Wounded Hussar

after the Dordan concert in Butler House, Kilkenny, January 1991

In another City nearly fifty
and that slow air tears my lungs
ageing backlit figure
in the shadows out of focus
some dark night outside
and time stops still – I am
the floating isolated skull
over there in the smoky corner
the faded picture on the poster
fallen down behind the till
still looking out for love

Cold and listening to music
slow air and punctured lungs
plans shelved again and
folded up in Rand McNally
that woman in Chicago
who slept with a loaded gun –
have I somehow outlived them all
the lovers and the drunks
and all my dispossessed
my own poor lost hussars at one
with moonlight and blue music

Music in the air tonight
that slow air tears my lungs
and women comb the killing fields
to find dead lovers news of men

stretched naked in the streets
so cold so white as ice tonight
beneath the Precinct wall
along the levee and the slips
on the river-walks and quays
by this salt fatal river –
this landlocked frozen sea

Trapped until Winter cracks
in the ice outside your door
tomorrow morning I will ask –
St Brigid's Day the first of Spring –
which road to take to catch
my nineteen-forties distant self
walking in unfamiliar snow
the sting of sea foam in my mouth
rock salt in the fields – tonight
this same slow air is yours
this slow air fills the room

Blood-Red Flowers

I thought it was another country
and I find it is
another country of the blood-red flowers
here in your rainswept house
Semitic characters in chalk
still linger on the gate-post
not washed away by the wind and rain –
through the same distorting lens
of leaded glass I see
mad creatures climb the garden wall

And finding out again again
that no one constitutes a harbour
just another afternoon of rain
and turning round and round
in an inflammatory circle – so
to pick up all the pieces now
whose job is that? To sort
through all this durable detritus
these weary sentences
those unfinished bits of glass

With no names engraved thereon
that's it? I should have given up
on it? Long since? You think?
Kept one eye always on the clock and left
before the neon lights came on
been ready to accept the gifts
of emptiness and avocado stones
and then put on my hat and coat
to follow the French accordeon
out again past the edge of town

Should have done but didn't
not even when the set collapsed
and the rustic roof fell in
in a shower of Tarot cards
with the balcony in bits I was
still the stroller on the boulevard
lost in that El Paso game of dice
looking for a way into your space
with no words left to say
still spinning to the end of play

And yet for us I never doubted
but that we are kindred in the skin
with all the same desires regrets
we can put on take off the secret parts
like gloves – in the park today
three figures called me in the rain
to join them in a shadow game
of moving on to answer
to the whisper on the phone –
I need to make you want to make
you come to me you'll come

Interior: The Great Fish

What fails me then to get to this
so empty – empty as an eggshell in the grass –
but May again triumphalist?
Laburnum lilac chestnuts dust
the gutters of the sunlit road
another year has come and gone
and Niall just turned nine
he tells me now is feeling almost ten:
fearful for the human heart
I try to put a gloss on this

And think of Dr Hook and Lucy Jordan
who'll never ride through Paris with
the warm wind in her hair –
this time in Paris last year
half-translated I sat down to make a note
in sunlight in the Rue Berzelius –
no bad thing either
to stop alone at some oasis –
holding a virgin telecarte
still hooked-up to the Universe

It's not enough but it may do
in time to put an edge on things
to find a way back in
without traduction – swamp creatures once
we now come down to water here
between the trees beside this pool
and make display of well-oiled parts:
among the bones and tracks of dinosaurs
we too can leave
the marks of marvellous birds

Distances: South Missouri, November 1991

Glimpsed from a Greyhound Bus
the eighteen-wheeler reads
Grief Brothers on the highway
and we're pitching down
Interstate 44 from St Louis
in the snow – driven
by a Born Again Christian
whose Night Rider eyes contain
the certainty of resurrection
beyond tomorrow and the bill-boards

Tonight I read-off history
reading off the magic names
rocketing past the Meramec Caverns
Six Flags Over Mid-America
Eureka Bourbon Cuba
Sullivan and Lebanon
Waynesville and Fort Leonard Wood
all Legend and the Legend is
Explanation of Symbols
or *How To Determine Distance*

Tomorrow or the next day
you will take me to a hidden place
of upland silences – the road
leads down into the lake
and we move off into the winter hills
to eat persimmons and black walnuts
looking south to Arkansas: in
recognition I salute these places –

say their names: *Manor Kilbride*
Moon City – Hollister
and *Poulaphuca Lacken* Branson

Distance And Funeral: Meath, December 1991

1.

The people here prehistory
who carved these stones
what messages and how to read them

Are only voices in the wind
the sound of rooks and daws
crow-sounds in winter

Are also all my childhood
the darkness and the dripping trees
grow brown and all around

Corroding mortar flakes
pieces slither from the walls
to crumble in the winter grass

2.

I am no longer part of this
but was I ever – did I ever fit
into my memory of how it was

Or is the restless movement all
returning home on spinning wheels
going back for funerals

Becoming part of life
half-way through unfinished stories
and called away before the end

3.

And yet – what messages
must be there in the genes what
blueprints from the distant people

The solar masons who
built permanence along the Boyne
and vanished into wind and rain

As you did too my Famine
ancestor – my travelling man from Cavan
who came here on a load of eels

And stopped and stayed and showed
us other passage graves to read
and other histories to learn

I feel the self-same touch
of hoarseness in my voice – the tell-tale
change of pace along the road

Another April: Father Hayden Bosheen

for Margaret Cosgrave

On the foot of your kind welcome back
I am walking in to the City happy
thankful and glad for Eve and the apple
at ease in Kilkenny in the evening sun
and pausing in St Patrick's Churchyard
mindful of times drinking wine by the neck
in graveyards or smoking long cigarettes
in graveyards or devouring Hoffman-LaRoche
until I become as invisible
as the children I hear at play – as unseen
as the bird that rustles in the tree above me
now all our names are weathered from the stones
and – as indication I am not a vampire
my shadow cast by the setting sun

Fidelities

Darkness initially and then
the same soft under-water focus
drifting weeds
a sea-cave lit by candles
and failing yet again to make a contact
once more I put the question
from twenty years before

What do you think of?
What goes on in there?

Nothing – she smiles –
nothing whatever: inside here
there is emptiness
all this is emptiness

In sudden neon lighting
she reconstructs a face

An emptiness of such complexity
that I am lost if I begin to think
and if that is what she chooses
to present
this enigmatic porcelain
who am I to disbelieve –
bring down upon my neck
some less acceptable dimension
of man or bird
yet another fall to earth
or any killing of your choice

Perhaps the pheasant
in the clothes-shop window?

It was in a mirror that I saw
so long ago so long ago
that intermittent flash of red
those flames that dance and lift –
the shower of sparks
on limbs that shift and fall
like logs on burning embers

Blues Note For John Jordan

from St James's Hospital, June 1992

Dear John – I miss you greatly
in pain and doped
last night in the William Wilde Ward
after surgery I slept
and dreamt of you
cruising Ireland in an open car
some timeless Summer in the 1950s
surrounded by friends and phantoms
with hampers bottles books
or sitting on a lawn recounting
stories without rancour
before you all moved on to view
the grey stone house in the meadow
lion and shells above the lintel
with no intention there of horror
haemorrage or shadow –
but time enough to think of that
when you come walking home from Santiago

I woke at six and all around
in daylight white as salt-flats
angels and poets were waking up
in hospitals and houses
just like everybody else
kicking aloft their heels and skirts
coming-to alone with others
or losing themselves in sex
discreetly in the suburbs
or shambling solitary

from gaps along the city quays
and open spaces of the Fifteen Acres –
clients of the morning shake
in early bars and railway stations
spin-drift drinkers
sea-pool creatures stranded

Clutching votes for Maastricht
some run aground at Dollymount
and some rise up with flocks of birds
to track across to Booterstown
or settle into Dublin 4
marching across the marshes
like frog-princes to the dogs
some learn like you the code of cloisters
discipline in laid-out books
while others find their own escapes
making vows of abstinence
in meeting-rooms in Aungier Street
and still the whirling city
floats in air
swaying waves of football crowds
come riding up the river Swan
from Shelbourne Road to Harold's Cross
new colonists from Bristol
quick-silver to the plimsol
sailing home on mercury
without the trick of Cocteau's gloves –
and *Orpheus Lives* in Effra Road

The room was bright with light
when I came back
post operative and slightly crazed
my life before my eyes

in shock half-naked lurching
from my bed to walk
St James's corridors alone
premonitory gatherer at fifty
flapping and hopping from crack
to crack – a solitary dancer
picking up my bits of bone
from furnaces and city dumps
split images and sleight of sound
dried streaks of blood
my broken bits of city speech –
In his last hours
the soldier with the bandaged head
heard voices from the street
a bas Guillaume a bas Guillaume
heard gulls and slogans
on the breeze *a bas Guillaume*
and *I'm for Europe*
slogans voices
gulls' voices in the wind
and I'm for Europe too
God knows: we never left it John
wandering here for forty years
as it goes on
in all its European contradictions –
the histories of Sarajevo
corpses at the gates of Moscow
churros at dawn among the dead
a sometime morning entertainment
on the roads around Madrid
the barbarous New Jerusalem
grown up across the water
status quo expedience
and that vindictive smiling

senile Master of The Rolls
Wehrmacht and Bundesbank
poison clouds above Kiev
Charlemagne and Stupor Mundi
the filthy bombing of Iraq
not the placard stuff of slogans
something to write home about
complacently –
remembering our own perspective
the only Post-Colonial
State in Western Europe –
your Western Europe –
remembering Dublin afternoons
upstairs rooms in empty colleges
dead souls dead unincluded souls
and all the dusty shelves
with rows of cardboard boxes
full of human skulls and bones
and human stories – stolen
shameful catalogues
of other plundered peoples

There is a wind of politics
a wind that blows about our walls
not just our European history
Hitler and St Francis of Assisi –
for all that we may walk today
in Harold's Cross among laburnums
from Sceilg Mhichíl to the Albaicín
do penance in Jerusalem
or make the journey from St Jacques
the pilgrim road to Santiago
with silver wings upon our heels
tomorrow in Bohemian Grove

or Berchtesgaden
or some other version of the Bunker
serious heads of state will sit
drinking from a human cup
without reflecting surfaces
Greek Fire or Pepper's Ghost
or the magician's smoky glass –
it will be real no artifice
no mime of tinsel there or heartbreak
but toasts to commerce and to murder
drinking to the dispossessed
whose unforgiving skulls they use
Ai Ai Hieronymo
Ai Ai Alhambra

And still we carry on
while there is sunlight in the corridor
the news ticks in piles up
from all points of the compass –
The winter will be hungry
and the hard winds blow
But none of this is news to you
old hand at hospitals
recidivist of love
highwire traveller at night
European tightrope walker
attender at infirmeries
astonisher and puzzlement
old mentor veterano Ветеран
in eight years more we're of an age
and never were too far apart
in eight years' time another date
another century at fifty-eight
a new millennium and gravitas

but you are gone and I must ask you this –
did St Theresa give a damn
for your discalcèd Indian?

The Paradise Sexy Shop

for Ian Campbell Ross

Driving from here to the city you will find
the Paradise Sexy Shop
just past the village of Strozzacapponi
not far from the Fairground
pick-up quarter – when the moon is right
lights glitter on the roundabout
and cars slow down pull up take off

Eiléan and Niall have gone to the fair
to celebrate the *Fiera dei Morti* –
tonight or tomorrow we'll be eating
fave dei morti with apples and nuts:
but for now my son is sailing in the *Barca*
Halloween is hanging from the rafters
and the ship flies up and up

In Peredelkino among the leaves
Lev Oshanon eighty – five times married
Soviet balladeer lover and poet
is putting the last fine cut
to his life and work: *A Half a Century
of Love Betrayal Jealousy* –
he dedicates it to his present wife

You should have come here when you drank
he says – and gives us Volga carp and vodka
apple-juice fire and welcome – two musicians
play the words: *when I think of all
the women who have loved me*

151

in that poisoned day
then I remember the woman I betrayed

There is a filament that runs through this
the central nervous system of a fish –
I do not see the patterns in the fire
I see the fire itself and that's enough:
for we are human and we could be doing worse
than driving half across the world to find
the Paradise Sexy Shop

School Bus: Via Cigne

On my first day back from Russia
I walked down to the road to meet you
coming home on the school Pulmino

Glad to be home wherever home is
benign in the present hour of grace
I wave to the children on the bus

Well Dad – you say – that's all right too
but you know how it is
there can be enemies on the bus

And yes I understand how that can feel
when you begin to be convinced
either that you are somehow alien

Or that all the others on the bus
your fellow travellers themselves
have come from outer space

Sometimes it happens in the middle
of the night – when you discover
that there's no one else on the ship

Just you and the lights burning
the engine throbbing and those dark
patches in the corridors:

A blazing ship full of people
passing the Lizard at midnight
and there's no one there at all

Acorns From Pavlovsk

for Eugenia Alexandrovna Ravtovich

For so long and so often
it seems to be a race
against something:
trying to get back to the angel
before the fuel runs out –
Burning the wheel-house
in mid-Atlantic
or running against time
lungs hope or drink

Where are you
oh secret lovers?
We send out letters
no one answers
Where are you
Dead Fathers?
Where are you
oh railway stations?

Then somewhere on the journey
it all comes simpler:
a porcupine feather
two white snail-shells
in my garden
walnuts from the tree
in late October –
and in my pocket
these five acorns
I have carried from Pavlovsk

Night Sounds

This is what I do these marks upon a page
is what I do and all I do
and I am caught here fighting with it – fighting
with myself with interruptions and with silence
finding messages and wondering what's the use:
a wind that howls about the house
could bring me home
the stream that breaks its banks at night

Can bring me nowhere: the hunger that I need
escapes into the rotting leaves
beneath the walnut tree: spurious warmth of ash:
again I fear I have lost touch with language –
can answer only now to touch itself
and half-remembered images and music: did I not
go deep enough into that same morass
to bring back music? Bring you back?

Went back among the dead to tell it:
and found my father threatened by Hibiscus
drenched with whiskey howling in his sleep:
nightly wrestling with the moon – the moon
of Jacob's Ladder or the truth below:
downstairs the dreadful sisters taking root –
night visitors with barbers' knives
rehearsing their persuasions for the wake –

Landscape and history: unhappiness does not
come into it – that's how it was
at best refusing to renegue on faith –
observing some appointed trust: at worst

155

not ripping tongues from rusty bells
living in the fire and not the flame
drinking slanted sunlight from the well
not falling to the bottom of the lake –

Tonight the distant lights are quiet:
moon and time have run aground – my household
here in sleep has worn away the circuits
thrown damp grass and salt upon the fire
and still it moves: just outside this house
my far out furthest planet from the Sun
new-born new-launched Galileos
drift unseen past the shutters of my room

A Map of Valentine 1993

Yesterday on St Valentine's Day
all the birds of the townlands
chaffing in the trees
talking and choosing the season's mate
was also the Feast of the Cats
biding their time to speak
and seen from this end of the valley
improbable between the olives
Panicale loops like a Bristol Bridge
suspending its fret-saw stretch of sky
above the lake's reflected light
Città della Pieve to my left
in the mist – where the Sacristan
waits for unwary women –
adjacent Missiano sinks into the fields
astray behind me Tavernelle
and on my right skirts lifted
Colle Calzolaro bares its backside
to St Valentine's sun and me
to the steamy new ploughed panorama
and the far-flung stretching farms
And God in His Heaven but it's good to be
even a part in the sum of this
in this valley that spins about
in the temporary Winter heat
stung by the midday breeze that blows
from the furthest hills and snow –
curving purple shifting hills
whose folds of shadow emphasise
the sex and bush of far-off pines –
                    and it's good
to be walking across St Valentine's map
heavy with light and Spring and blood

Fire And Snow And Carnevale

In winter fire is beautiful
beautiful like music
it lights the cave –
outside the people going home
drive slowly up the road – the strains
of phone-in Verdi on the radio
three hours back a fall of snow
sprinkled the furthest hill
where clouds have hung all winter

The day gets dark uneasy
dark and darker still
and you little son come home
riding the tail of the wind
in triumph – tall and almost ten
with confetti in your hair
home successful from the carnevale
with your two black swords
and your gold-handled knife

I feel the chill and hear
the absent sound of snow
when you come in –
white fantastic scorpions spit
in the fiery centre of the grate
plague pictures cauterised –
In winter fire is beautiful
and generous as music – may you
always come this safely home
in fire and snow and carnevale

The Gourmands Of Europe

for Nathalie Peyret

Sometimes this year I see
the greed of Empire
here in the house and Burke and Hare
at large in the kitchen –
Archduke Rudolfo him
turned into a plant
turned green beyond osmosis

Turned into vegetable
fruit and cereal
those are grapes that were his eyes
red-faced from ingesting
he bobs among tomatoes
his forehead polished
to the texture of apples

Apricots corn and wheat
form the substance of his cheek
his ear a handsome mushroom
supports a bursting fig –
his jewellery passion-fruit
plums and raisins
hazel-nuts and nectarines

The Adam's apple is a pear
his furnace mouth
a full-fleshed chestnut
jumping from its spiky rind
brings air and pasta

to the bubbling lungs
of truffle oil and aubergines

He talks of food
throughout Affairs of State –
the rebel pepperoncino
sly mango wily marrow-flower
yams pulses peas courgettes –
all he has swallowed up
all he still hopes to eat

And God do I not sometimes long
to hear of something else?
To hear some news
of snipe or curlew
corn-crake cuckoo bittern thrush
or even maybe once to hear
of birds that sing in Berkeley Square

Irish Seed-Potatoes

1.

They won't grow there my neighbour said
in April – no foreign thing
will ever grow in the soil of Umbria

The Roman tried and we told him –
besides it is too early hereabouts
to think of planting seed-potatoes

And furthermore the moon is growing:
no seed will take
that is not planted in the shrinking moon

2.
At the start of May I pause a moment
in the cool after thunder
to admire their sharp-green stalks

Flourishing beside the vines – I am
thinking of Ireland and trying to return
to a message for my father

Begun when we came face to face
in the Achill house of Heinrich Böll
twelve months ago last March

Begun and lost in moving on from there –
to Dublin Moscow here
carrying these pages round

Repeating conversation with the past –
trying to keep perception bright
like putting sea-light under glass

3.

Until today I find myself at last
beside the corner of the tillage
reading Thomas Kinsella's anthology

Comforted by these few stalks
and recognising differences – somehow always
exiled stranger to my own

As if I had not served my time
sheltering in the clefts of rocks.
on sodden hills where no sun shines

Coughing in foggy mail-boat mornings
labouring on foreign sites
and flying home at every chance

Enough to be here now and trying to write
a message for my wandering father
in whatever language fits –

Fits this and fits the journeying itself:
the starving freight of coffin-ships
and the wasting death of Goll Mac Morna

March In Dublin – Return Journey

for Michael Hartnett

At eleven o'clock
in the morning
that's how I found him
standing and gesturing
like a mad waiter –
and from his pockets
spoons knives and forks of words
flying in all directions

And on the floor
in the public bar
lying down in the middle of the room
his *compañero* roaring
in black leather trousers
toenails painted red
how he dare not go a-hunting
for fear of little men

And oh my friends
from that far country
I know what pains you took
to get here –
long long trains with buffet cars
years spent
in the holds of cattle boats
haunted nights in railway stations

Above Pesaro: June 1993

Nothing cleans the ground
said the Padrone of the Villa Ernestina
that evening above Pesaro – nothing cleans
the ground but planting *erba medica:*
and nothing clears the mind say I
but moving on: putting the wheels
in gear and moving on

And coming down at last
in sun and thunder from the Appenines
with our share of chest-pains
and the engine full of air
that's how we came to be here
oil blowing-out the dipstick
leaving a trail of thinning tar
that petered out in heat in Novilara
and that's how we come to be here
in the functional shade at noon
beneath the mediaeval tower
built by this man's father's father
to give a prospect of the sea –
Stranger than the Cyclops eye
of Military Intelligence
in Crossmaglen
Improbable as San Gimigniano

And what did we ever claim to be
in all our caravanserai
run so ragged on our journeys
climbing up to all these hill-towns
but *seme di pioppi* – poplar seeds

that drift across the valleys
bell-sounds on the necks of horses
on treeless plains above the timber line –
people of the high fields
travellers of the wandering rocks
with tongs and cauldron?
Who did we ever claim to be
but the stories we carry with us –
half of the cake with my blessing
or the whole of the cake with my curse

And happening here by chance at last
without the benefit of clock or compass
was nothing more
than falling into Prospero' s garden
familiar recognised surprises
like hearing the whistle blow
on the far off cars of the night-train
for real for the first time
when I woke for a moment
turning in sleep in Milford
Michigan – or here today
among pines and palms and wild asparagus
watching the ships below
tacking along the wind to Venice
remembering the letters of Aretino
where murder and money and dust are real
as chance encounters in the street
or revisiting the Magic Mountain
climbing up again through
shaky mornings in the Rif
or standing in a wind-scrubbed square
in shock at evening in Urbino
dazed by the light beneath the walls

of the Dukes of Monte Feltro
and hoping to go home again
to settle into stone-flagged kitchens
to be welcomed into conversation
in houses that are gone –

To be going home like Marco Polo
To be going home like Carolan

2.

Memory is a heavy coat
worn sometimes back to front
against the rain: I see
my mother's father on an open road
dead before I was born

Walking a hundred years ago
and wonder if I've dressed him right
in hard-hat frieze-coat
waist-coat watch and chain
walking homeward from the town

Against the wind and rain-
washed countryside of Land Disputes
eviction emigration – the world outside
the walled-in trees and deep
solidified demesnes of Meath

He stayed when others left
for Melbourne Perth and San Francisco
leaving me a place unoccupied
a track worn down across the fields
a photograph I shelter from the light

Some little roads with weary ghosts
a well that might run dry
broken china in the garden
a settle-bed that's long since empty
all the ticking turned to dust –

Memories of childhood –
pink roses on the kitchen delph
and that's how frail we are
too quick to anger – so defenceless
in our seasons and so easy to break up

3.

Even without the nightingales
these women in the summer garden
of Augusta's house
Augusta Giorgia Mariamne
make up the persons of a Tragic play
while in the wings
a tableau from a photograph
five others dressed in crinolines
provide a chorus tint of sepia
gathered timeless at the gate
waiting for the messenger –
the dogs are sleeping in the shade
each symbol in its place
and every boy of ten
in leather sandals
could be Orestes or Telemachus

There are no mirrors here
except the hazy random sea

no lake of metal open to the sky
breaks up the pattern of the hills
and clouds and mountains to the south –
Fulvio – ten – is Giorgia's son
incumbent of the cryptic paths
those half-reclaimed and those
whose marble stones sink further down
into the earth – the Queen
his mother dark and Greek
a traveller from a curving vase
whipped from the House of Atreus
and brought here from Cattolica –
a movement of matt wax at night
and dressed in black
she glides among the trees and tables

Once more the King is missing
from the picture – gone to Thebes
Protector of The Buttock-Fields
on one of the beaches far below
his waking hours are passed
in the muster stretch and catch of thongs
about the legs and crotch –
here the humming garden sings
throughout the afternoon
and every boy of ten
becomes in turn Ajax or Achilles –
another sighting of the Fleece
beyond the Adriatic
some further news of Thrace
a severed head falls from a tree
wrapped up in leaves and dill
a figure hanging from a butcher's hook
and another piece of shrapnel
comes bursting from the lamp

4.

The mythologies that families weave
to hold themselves together –
Your house has burned down
and *You've* no home to go to
my one-legged uncle's nautical academy
shelled at random by the Helga

Crossed legends
of the great cook and the heroic drinker
or the alcoholic painter
whose fingers never shook –
I had a message here today
a slogan on a cup – it read:
the geography of yearning

Lily Dunne in her apron strings in Dublin
walking around the snug
on wires like a crab in the sun

oh the nerves missus
the nerves oh the nerves missus
the nerves the nerves the nerves

And did the drowned man
have his arms across his chest in resignation
or was he fighting still for air?

And what of me – sitting here
in this conservatory
waiting for the wind to hit
the hanging chimes again
and reading over-and-over the legend
of Blood Fish and Bone

5.

This was the summer of the year I hoped
to open out the rann
to reach the place beyond mythologies

To see the monsters all unmasked
moving further into age
where one can make admissions without guilt

The summer of the year I built
my four-square shelter in among the trees
beneath some oaks upon a terraced hill

The year I tied back thorns
and cut away the undergrowth
to make a gap for sunlight to come through

And this was my retreat – five upright
posts of heavy chestnut
the roof was reed-canes from the lake

Laid on rafters from a ruined house –
for furniture a table chair
and hammock for the evening sun

And like an aging Satyr gone to seed
among the trees
half visible against the light on leaves

I came to be acquainted with the wood
crab-apples falling on my roof
small creatures dropping from the oaks

The daily flight-path of the clouds
drifting over from the lake
and all the noise and uproar

Along the forest floor – the slow
smooth rustle of a snake
sliding up against the bank

Quick crash of lizards
through the brittle crust – the
sudden cries of goats alarms of birds

Flying ants and stinging flies
and children's voices on the breeze
came with the drifting poplar seeds

This was the summer of the year
that Niall learned Italian
and learned to beat the video games

In Carlo's pizzeria –
took up karate fell in love
and all the other rites of passage

Appropriate at ten – the year
the post-colonialists arrived
to turn us into Tunbridge Wells

And this was our retreat –
forced out and on the road again
in flight we gave up argument

Seeing who the monsters were –
in argument we can persuade ourselves
that we are surer than we are

6.

What a way to present yourself
said the Doctor
when I got the clapped-out
twenty hundredweight van to Dublin
against the odds –
what a way to present yourself
he repeated
looking down from the fourth
floor of his script
lifting his shoulders and lighting
a Freudian cheroot

Did he think I'd been rehearsing
all the road up from the South?

But that fish this morning
on the lake
breaking the under-surface of the mist –
does a fish present itself
when it leaps?
That dead bird
beneath the Church at Aghabog –
or that long-shadowed walker
that struts beneath my window?

And am I not always listening
over the noise of the engine
for other voices –
other invitations home?
Are you lost are you lost – and
how should I know till I get there?

Did you meet anyone on the road?
I did
And did they ask you anything?
Yes they did
And what did you tell them?
Nothing! Nothing! I told them nothing!
Told them nothing? Good!

7.

What was going on there when the light
became so bad I couldn't see
what we were eating? I was preoccupied

About how carelessly those people came
from Iron Bridge or Tunbridge Wells
and thinking of Ó Bruadair

Is mairg nach fuil 'na dhubhthuata,
Cé holc duine 'na thuata,
ionnas go mbeinn mágcuarda

Idir na daoinibh duarca: Into
the second week of June – I wrote –
and all the bright days pass

But not with any record of their going –
our sceptred islanders are back
in occupation – landed wearing GB plates

With Marks and Spencer bags
a weekly pre-paid order for The Telegraph
and sacks of charcoal *Packed In England*

Our super-market pilgrims
have turned us into playtime once again
and little since is actual – they

Spend a half hour at the flower-bed
every morning – an outing to the shops
at ten o'clock

Then home preparing lunch
with glass in hand – and when we eat
before we do the clearing up

The making of the next meal has begun
until one day of incidental sun
becomes another and now May itself is gone

A haze of Sunday Supplement observance –
outdoor cooking tasting wine
amusement at the quaintness of the neighbours

Unable to speak normally to children
but lavishing affection on the cat –
and yet you say they're decent people

For all the drinking and the greed
they don't give in to sweat or indolence
are not consumed by alcohol or guilt

Just killing time with tedium
and pouring good days after bad – eating
sleeping filling empty bottles up

And looking sad-eyed at the world
till all our waking hours begin
to seem like sleeping with the enemy

And here the enemy is weariness –
The weariness I always felt
each time I passed through Crewe going South

That undirected rage and puzzlement –
there's some agenda here
I cannot get a grip of – some settled arrogance

That keeps them safely from the edge –
among the blood-red flowers I note
the icons of our histories

Colonial and colonised:
the stuff of pomp and circumstance
angels of an iron age

Plantation symbiosis

8.

Today the day after rain
in recollection
I am listening
to the new-washed sounds of birds
trying out the air again
and thinking – this misdirected anger
ill-becomes me

Given sanctuary we all should be
as generous as birds –
like deer upon the avenue at night

lift up the rann
rise up the air and open it out

But this is not a fairy-tale
and did you know that I had met
a witch here once –
a vampire child with a machine gun
who blew everyone away?
Who set out to show me
we own nothing
least of all time and space

But what else have we got –
what have we got if not
space and history
and the stories we carry with us

I have a store of baggage too
rise up the air and open it out

Did I not tell you that I met
a witch here once?
A white-haired woman
in a long black coat
nodding and dancing among the trees –
who set out to show me
we own nothing
least of all time or space

not time or space
or nakedness
not even owning the air we breathe
owning nothing

Having no control over others
not smiles or whispers
or night-time quickness of breath

not even an instant shared
we own nothing
    neither ourselves
    nor touch
nor the momentary sounds of birds

and that was the bleakest of times
rise up the air and open it out

And in this day – is this the day
some Sunday maybe
is this the day it starts?
So hard to tell where histories begin –
when some cell thinks
to go askew within the blood –

Or that figure
nodding and dancing on the hill up there
among the trees?
Or only a wayward bush?

9.

So what kind of dualist are *you?* Barnet
agus Beecher Hedges *agus* Stowe
were somehow there at the start of it –

I remember the winter of 'forty-seven
rattling home from school on the tram
getting off at Holles Street

And peeing in the snow in Merrion Square
being five and sick and seeing
gigantic firelit aunts around my bed

Later when I was seven and well
I ran down a hill to my grandmother's house
through flying heavy country snow

The hunched green bus to Granard brought me
past humps of turf in the Phoenix Park –
turf we set to dry in the oven –

Staggering on through Dunboyne and Trim
past Walker's Georgian house and lands
and Parr's and Alley's and the Hill of Ward

Into Athboy and the dung-soiled street
to drop me down at Nugent's corner –
and I walked out of town on the empty road

Past the graveyard and up the hill
through hills themselves beyond horizons
to the hens that clucked in the yard

To my grandmother's fire and glass of port
and salty bacon on a chimney-hook –
to the fire where she aired her shrouds

And the daily prayers she offered up
for the canonization of Oliver Plunkett
and three days' warning of death –

And whatever else might chance to pass
in our weather-soaked world – where ghosts walked
along the roads at night

Cries of vixens echoed in the dark
with news of neighbours' loss
or accidents that happened in Australia

While round and round and round in Dublin
thirty children in a circle
sang and marched about the room

York Road Dun Laoghaire 1947
and an autocratic hand beat time on a piano
How many kinds of wild-flowers grow

In an English Country Garden
I'll tell you some of the names that I know
and the rest will surely pardon – my

Fellow victims of paralysis and Empire
Kingstown Grammar they called the school
at the end of the Free-State tram

That brought us daily to Dun Laoghaire
and I read the Bible and Death of Nelson
with Armstrong Ireland Goodman Devlin

Goodbody Draper Gentleman Long
and my mother worked to teach us Gaelic
Republican and pluralist

Cumann na mBan with the same beliefs
that sixty troubled years ago
cost her a teaching post in Dundalk –

Today in Monaghan and looking down
from this Big House upon the lake and garden
gauging the familiar rain

The turning of the season and the leaves
with my own fifty years between
it seems appropriate and almost unimportant

Except that all the women I have known
were singular – my mother and her mother
and all the women who have worked these hills

Were singular and real:
I think of the *vicina* in the white house
across the road in Umbria

The way she walks on broken ground –
through geese and clamps and binder-twine
as self-contained about her business

As sure of hammer sickle scythe

10.

We have been
living with strangers
idir na daoinibh duarca
our partners in this house who said –
The Irish? I mean even so and if
we gave the Irish their freedom now
they wouldn't know what
to do with it ... would they?
Would they? They wouldn't
know what to do with it ...

O Heart of Mockery
does nothing ever change
and how often do we have to see
this same boorish scene repeated
this manic arrogance?
Hard-money heroes coming-on
like Superman in Moscow

and Audie Murphy always
striding through Saigon –

And we continue trying to avoid
some half-cocked confrontation
with the grievance that is history
polite and liberal and angry –
but the truth is

I was almost driven mad by rage
anger at brutality in uniform
and out of it
at shootings at Loughgall
bombings in Warrington
at murder in the streets
angry for the dispossessed
and the homeless on the Underground
angry with complacency
and the pietistic rule of law and order

Angry at jejune Revisionists
as at ill-informed intransigence
at good poetry in bad translation
angry with committee-men
calling in on self-promotion
angry with sleeveens
obsequious and reverential
at funerals the morning after
when embarrassments have been
disposed of decently
and safely laid to rest

Angry with the grunt and
duck-billed platitude

that telegraph the Tory message
and all lick-spittle merchants
touters of received opinions
and received pronunciations
angry at over-simplifiers
canting boors and bully-boys
and anyone who takes
common human courtesy for weakness

And I am angry still
angry with myself
for being there at all
angry with myself for keeping silent
angry with my memories
of taking to the hills
angry with myself
for wasting time in folly
angry with myself in truth –
and this is folly too
angry pointlessly with you
for not being someone else

11.

Where did you go dead fathers
we send out letters no-one answers
Niall son we are I think
mad parachutists
dropping through a tiny patch of sky
and landing nowhere –
that's who we are
people of the Ice Queen
the sunset

and the Hag of Beare
that's what we have become
where did you go dead fathers
out past the morning ships
leaving me here on the shore

When I was twelve or so
in Blackrock Baths
a naked man attacked me once
he spat and said – you
you're cultured Irish
you play the harp –

What hidden businesses
were going on there?
What contorted angers
hatred and disgust?

where are you gone dead fathers
who walked on empty Sunday paths

Oh child I wish that I did –
and if only he knew the half of it
where are you now dead fathers
who understood music and numbers

This time last year
standing in the dark in Moscow airport
at the baggage carousel
I met a woman in a stetson
an urgent messenger from home
who said –
          You know? In the madhouse
the general opinion was – and

this they consoled themselves with —
that whatever about the rest
there was one —
there was one who hadn't a hope
in hell
      not a hope in hell
not a hope not one
      of coming through —
      and that was you

where did you go dead fathers
who understood poetry — life without hope
or did she think I hadn't noticed?

Son did I tell you
one time I was happiest?
In the Krassikov's orchard
out past Tchekova
digging a hole in the Russian earth
turning over the Russian earth

without thought
      just that
digging a hole for rotten apples
digging a hole among the birches

12.

When will we set out again
to look for Craggaunowen?
Or can such sudden
rightness be repeated?

To be going home like Marco Polo
Coming home like Carolan
That red leaf
on the steps of the big stone House
such a sudden splash
of scarlet –
the outline of a snow-flake
starfish and anchor

The crystals call us back
and the leaves
that fall into our rooms at night

But call us back to what – to sit
at the foot of the stairs
in the hall composing
farewells to music and to poetry

And we come back from wandering
to find ourselves foreign
foreign to the streets of childhood
new buildings fill the gaps
in memory – new voices words and accents
occupy our thoughts

Children grow that much bigger
that much older
in this Republic of the Mind
we carry with us
there is no preventing
new alliances of monsters
the idiot jeers that echo
from the school-yard
or the terrible simpering faces
of people who were young with us

You find that you have
spent your life
fighting with monsters
arguing one agenda
discussing one set of problems
sorting out one situation
until all-and-nothing changes

Not easy to be fluid
as Ivan Malinovski was
as I saw him here
in front of the fire
in Selskar Terrace
untouched and strange
in knee-length britches
speaking Critiques for Himself –
and even if one were
we don't have another lifetime
for a second run at it

Maybe that's why the
Jesuit student of metaphysics
hoping for poetry
made all his notes in prose
a mistake a mistake

With one chance only
to hit the plateau of desire
I can go back in time
and just for now –

Stopped on suspicion
by the police in New Ross
Washed away by the rain

before welcome in West Cork
Best of MacElligott's
welcomes in Kerry
Warmth and shelter in Kilkee
before the sea froze over

Stung by the wind
above Loop Head – now
your grandson sits beside me
as we drive the empty
road for Ennis
drinking Seven Up
eating a pizza –
and what are we doing
but looking
looking for the country
where we are not foreign

rolling in the Van
with the windows open
and together
we're searching for Craggaunowen

Jumping To The Loop

1.

Come all of ye latter-day
Journalists judges

Economists newspaper-
Columnists sophists

Broadcasters teachers
Doctors and gamblers

The middle-class ethos
I sat with in school

Is it true something new
May be coming this way

That the weather has changed
And the wind turned about?

Is it so is it so
In the red month of May?

Or sold downstream
Again oh my dark Rosaleen

With poisoned blue air
And oil-heaving sea?

God help us alannah
No sense in the story

Good money in England
And wine on the deep

Isn't this how it is
Isn't that how it was

For as long as
We've all been around?

That's too long Mac Dara
That's too long ago

You're lost in the time
Of the wicked old men

Fanatical men
With bellowing voices

Old arrogant men
Who sent youths out to die

But now we're hooked into
The thinking of Europe

Though I fear the new right
May come into its own

When occasion demands it
We'll rewrite the slogans

There's political clout
In negating the past

Bonnie Charlie himself
Has landed in Dublin

Two centuries late
And we've washed off the slate

The wide men in suits
Keep coming up roses

This trip to Damascus
And no questions asked

2.

Today looking over
The ocean to Tarbert

Considering all the way
Out to the Loop

How North African dope
Floats in on the beaches

Where help never came
From Prince or from Pope

How the Polis and Excise
Directing the seizures

Don't leave us a morsel
For symbol or toke –

When the continents drift
What foundation is left

What reality's left
When identities shift

Or what's at the end of
The movement of peoples

But to lie at the edge
Of a field in a ditch?

And when my time is come
I won't hang around

On the day I turn sixty
I'll leave for the south

To lean on a wall
At some wide river's mouth

In a westerly wind
In a blizzard of doubts

To keep my own die-hard
Appointment with – no

But I swear that
I'll be there and wait

For the end to approach me
In bed or stone boat

That is all by my oath
But I ask:

Will it make its way in
By the palm of my hand

Or the hole
In the horn of my foot?

Thinking Of May 1994: From Moveen West In The County Clare

for Thomas Lynch

1.
All that fortnight I was waking up
to bird-song early in the Post Bellum South –
all night the trains on the Norfolk Southern
cut slow tunnels through the dark
and the sound of swings and children's voices
from Walter Ollte's across the road
came to me cool after breakfast –

The end of April on Walpurgissnacht
I found a place to sit
beneath a Maple and a Tulip tree
all afternoon the heat climbed up
and unfamiliar flowers dropped like fruit
hot strong and sweet as tea at a fair –
confusing geographies and language
in the smell of white-pine boxwood briar
the countryside had caught me on the hop

As in the Ozarks too it caught me
the panoramic lake and trees
called up Italian sounds and voices
archipelagoes of Archimago – the eerie image
of a bathing pool with no one there
and I
not having the questions to put
yet alone being able to interpret answers
as blind as the next at Newgrange

Without the history of townlands
I cannot scan the landscape
and what's left becomes
a series of synapses: of why
I didn't make it to the Jesse James Museum
to read a poem in South Missouri
for Jesse and the boys like Vera Lynn –
too chary maybe of cant or kitsch
of tying yellow ribbons and the rest?
Too superior by half: by half not good enough

The mind picks up on what it can – and I
see Tchekov's workplace here
by the lake at Table Rock
in the little wooden bell-tower
of the sundeck of a herb-farm – and in Virginia
the lines of the Gazebo on the lawn
before the timbered house at Mount San Angelo:
in Tchekova that's also how it is
a yachting superstructure
improbably set inland among trees – a
landlocked photograph:
his postcard –
My home where I wrote The Seagull

2.

Time and a little space
is all our statutory need – a little
time and warmth and those
appointments that we do not keep
admissions that we do not make to Immigration
the carnage at the river

in the dark parts of the mind
the long compulsion to the cliff path
and in St Isaac's Square St Petersburg
the poet dangling
terror
in the Hotel d'Angleterre

The seabird swims in air
we move in time and memory
with moments shared of history and focus
ambushed by perception:
perhaps a woman laughing in the doorway
of a Moscow block of flats at night
among October trees on Lenin Heights –
at once
significant and meaningless
as sunlit sparks of rain that sting
my window-pane today in Co Clare

For nothing is as is
what's real stays real despite revision –
the human form blends into landscape
and reverse –
a red bird burning in a bush
and how sensuous become the hollows
in the prairie of the belly
the roll of haunches curving into shadow
that fringe of hair beside the lake
the thrust of wind through pinions

as we fly out to sea
at last
carefree above the precipice
the thrust of wind through pinions

1995 – 2006

Street Scenes: The Ranelagh Road

The elderly man who sits
in the sun today
in Manders Terrace
is the same
who called at my door
last year with news of birds

Without preamble:
the swans are dying he said
when I opened the door –
gesturing into the air
the swans are dying
oh God the swans
the swans the swans the swans

Today it's the rats
are the trouble: the rats
hereabouts who live
in the trunk of a hollow tree

The rats and also another
old man
who pushes a bike
up the Ranelagh Road –
and I haven't seen him for weeks
he says not for weeks
have you? Have you seen him
or where could he be?

He's a skilled man too
he says – for he took a plant

one day like that one there
took out the knife
squinted along the length of the stick
sharpened the ends
and fashioned
a handle like you'd get on a hurley

But what would he want
with that? What would
he want that for?

And I don't know he
answers himself –
but a skilled man surely
and I haven't seen him this month or so
though I travel a lot myself
and I see him sometimes
in Sandymount
for that's where he sleeps you
know
in Sandymount there by the sea

And a skilled man surely –
but what would he want
with a stick like that?
With the two ends sharp
like that –
and a handle like
you'd get on a hurley?

For Pat Kaufman: Maker

Last night I saw the mist
lit up around the Empire State
and thought of you
finding your sense in shapes
in distance and perspective
in collage
                    blue lights
above the street
and images that shift
from the familiar to the strange
however many times I look

and this is how it was
a dinner that we ate Eiléan and I
in a restaurant
in Cardinal Lemoine
the death-bed house of Paul Verlaine

Le mystère?
enfin c'est Le Mystère
and then when I ordered it
                    the mystery ran out:
plus de mystère
the waiter said
Ie mystère n'existe plus

in the room beneath the room
where Verlaine died

Last night I saw the mist
around the Empire State lit up

with greens and blues
and shapes
from the other side of sleep

and thought of you
at work
and poems yet to make

the mystery still exists I thought
the mystery exists all right

Pensando Leopardi

1.

On the far side of
the mountain
climbing the stony path
I heard your voice
electric
well-remembered
hard-t accent
filling the space at noon
calling me north
to sea and slip
calling me back
to the stony beach

Maga Circe
word and voice: –

This is the fold in time
and here the hole in the rock
let you make life
and music start again
if there be music left
If I have music left

I have come so far
from the sea –
let there be music left

2.

Have I been
misled by the map –
my August tracks
are where
at last the world dries up –
I love the light
and dust
the now of things
of heat-cracked earth
loose piebald quills of porcupines
across the path
and down below
the harvest sunflowers
burnt to black

Up here
the macchia remains
my sun-dried
underwater garden –
the mountain too an island
full of voices
until walking over
all these hills
and keeping silence
itself appears invented purpose
that we survive
keep faith –
that there be music left

3.

The orioles return
each year
to light among the figs
... and I
have come so far
from the sea
blue sloes line the ditch
oak apples strew the path
and all I have done
with my summer days
is walk and think and walk –
if nothing
comes of nothing
can nothing come of this
nothing come of nothing
and let there be music left

Circe

The shadow
on the lung
I knew
was there reveals
the shadow

The shadow
in the brain
is real
and grows
and daily tells

The shadow
in the heart
is hot and red
is blood
bright blood

The shadow
on the road
is sudden
hard and quick
take care

The shadow
beating
in the thighs
remains always
the shadow

The shadow
waiting in the sky
anneals
restores us
to the sun

Three Sonnets

1 – Cladnageeragh

Wish the heron well for me
the curlew in the rain
and the kestrel on the wind
wish them well for me do
the gulls at their moorings
sheep in the ring-fort
boats taking shelter
and shrubs of the storm-break

As the moon to the sea
is the hare on the mountain
my heart to him too
small un-named creature –
free to go where the road goes
under the lights of your house

2 – December 31st 1998

For a moderate while there
fifteen years or so
I had a notion
of what was going on –
But now I'm afraid
it's Planet Pluto again
time for me to be moving
further and further out

Back to my lump of dusty ice
beyond the point of vision
in the meantime
I have to keep walking
talking making notes
calibrating the tilt of the telescope

3 – For Mairead and Paddy Lineen at Christmas

Blue white and red
are the sheep in the road
at Corrymore –
blue white and red
chrysanthemum sheep
of the Marseilleise
and the French Republic:
tricoloured partisans

And is that not the cup
of the winds up there
where water is moving light
and rustle of grass and scratch
of feather on rocks
carved out by time and ice

Tierra Del Fuego

for Kate Newmann

I walked across to the island
carrying sand and fire –
breathing the sulphur
of dead volcanoes hearing
the morning cock at the cross-roads
echo of gulls on salt-flats
echo of dogs across the ice-floes
dogs with yellow teeth
nothing moved in the ice-world
nobody called in the wind

None from before the guns and plague
people of snow and fire
from before the spillage for gold
before the orders to shoot on sight
before the agent posted the notice
A Pound for an Indian's Ears
Two pounds for an Indian Woman's Breasts
before words caught in the throat
what birds flew in the hail then
what did we see looking North

Our fires that were not beacons
people of fire we were –
to be discovered and displayed
naked against the light
in the ring in an iron cage
and space alone is left
in middens of food and ash –

only the odd bleak mound
of oyster shells and bones of birds
and ice and wood and rock
what was the sign by your foot
where was the lie of the path

All the howling night these waves
have crashed against the rocks
and rocks against the hills –
you on the bridge to the island walking
you lunar human naked bare
straining to see in the dark
what did the mirror show you
what did you see in the light

Stephen's Green: February 1998

Almost fifty years ago
that I sat here a child of six
dealing with the real –
the shadow on my lung
and the keeper with the stick
who ran to put me out

Thirty-five years since
I stood here – my arm
around a fair-haired girl
dealing with the real
and the keeper with the stick
who tried to drive us out

Today I sit here in the sun
dealing with the real
and the keeper with the stick
is nowhere to be seen –
this side of fifty years
he is younger than myself

Than all of my selves
I am older than the rocks
in the rockery-garden
older than the haunted head
of Mangan – older than
the angel waiting at the gate

Solstice

I brushed ashes
on the path today – swept powdered
bone into the cracks

Between
the brown silica bricks
beneath my feet

The city-garden bricks
of childhood
sunlight glinting quartz

Etched pictographs –
a rocky place suspended
in the mind at night

The same as when
apart we watched
the marvellous comet – above

A stony beach
for you – for me the sky at Easter
under Panicale ...

At Merrion Gates tonight
I watched the clouds outlined above
the hospital and sea

And further North
the nimbus Arctic-Circle light
affirming absences

And distance –
the empty space between the waves
that carry off the shore

As I brush ash and bone
into the path
push dust into the cracks

Cantejondo

I made my way to Mexico
through fields of biting rain

I saw a bird with wooden wings
saw sails that turned the wind

If I should wake tomorrow
to find the mountains gone

Could I make my way to Mexico
and the hall of the yellow sun?

The night I slept in Mexico
a blue bird on the wall

An Aztec moon with open eyes
was honey all night long

But morning came with ocean-light
and leached away the road

These nights I look for Mexico
my eyes the colour of blood

In Spello: Scáthach

Tonight
in Spello
before we go on stage
and looking eastward
to the hills
and Col Fiorito
earthquake country
I think of you
Scáthach

Sex and fire –
and how I might
come looking now
to find you
there
among the Sybils
if I'd the strength
to go back
forty years
and find us waiting

Comrade-
lover
from Sebastopol
my vendengeuse
copine
and fellow-traveller
so long ago
... *ou allez-vous comme ça* ...
in torn clothes
my old

co-veteran of distance
before the auto-routes

Those two
long since gone to ground
among mimosas

Old doors
have opened up
and closed
in Sainte-Geneviève
the police
have been and gone
the gutters
are clean
and the kerbs straight
and there isn't
a sign of us –
not an empty bottle
or broken boot
in sight

Just a cough
and catch of breath
today
in a room
on the plain below
Assisi:

a middle-aged man
in the afternoon
who clings to sleep
with
the shutters closed

Serial Flashback

I dreamt of drink again last night
of days in public houses without pause
and finding out the night's companions' names
the morning after in the hours
before the bars had opened up again –
I dreamt of this and spending years
remaining faithful to an act of hope
steering by unauthenticated stars
when others found out where the world begins
where people pay their way
foreclose on debt call in on favours done
die honoured in the end among their own –
I closed my eyes and set my sights upon
damp alleyways of Eden in the dawn

East Road East Wall

There was sunlight in the yard
when I broke my toe
five years of age
fifty years ago
in the hall the Japanese umbrellas
in the parlour
the mandolin and concertina
always sunlight in the yard
and heaps of coal
lights from the locomotives after dark –
I know
the heat from the fire-box glow
in Westerns

In the roof there were pointed windows
behind the house
the verandah
trainlines leading to the docks
down there where my green balloon
sailed off
all those missing years ago

And a journey with my mother
across Dublin
past the Custom House –
oh don't put me
in there – I said
don't ever put me in there –
three of us up
on a donkey and cart
moving my grandfather's piano

me and my mother
and the one-armed driver
my mother engaged –
piano-mover with a heart condition

Anchored in time
and light – a child
in Gandon's open space
where my
one-legged great-grand-uncle
navigated yet another
nautical academy

the first left sailing empty
abandoned in Belfast

Behind us all the afternoon
the East Wall in the sun
the parish register
of Lawrence O'Toole's –
recording the marriage of Wooloughan and Dias
and where was she from I wonder
the Iberian name at last
the further I go
the nearer I get
get back
                    to that peninsula
travelling South to Pembroke Street

Travelling now to
Clonskeagh
half a century later
across the river and city
across the Grand Canal
(that's my house there

in Ranelagh
that's where my son lives
and I
hold onto this
I think
and that is where I was born
down there
in Upper Leeson Street)

On the anniversary of my father's death
I am looking toward
Clonskeagh
where my mother is slowly dying
and saying her fragments of prayers
from childhood – oh
in this January month
as always
the trees are bare
I see too clear

In the pumping-station
I paused today
there was sunlight
in the yard
the engineer says
there is always sunlight here
he says –
not true I know
but I know what he means
for this was the place for photographs
on kitchen chairs
hauled into daylight
my people sat here
afternoons

This week
they begin to knock the house
that was Billy Woods's home:
and Norah Wooloughan's

the Japanese umbrellas
the mandolin and concertina
the columned clock on the mantel
their three sons

the heaps of coal
the puff and steam of locomotives
and the shaking great pump-engines
gone

outside the bricked-up
parlour window
a palm tree in the earth lives on

January 1999

Lobelias: Achill Island

for Donald Sur

A thousand flowers
lit up
the accidental roads

That brought us here
wherever
here is now –

Cool blue plaster
clusters
round the feet of saints

In empty childhood
country
churches long ago

Or green hydrangeas
in country gardens –
blue copper verdigris:

Korean blue and green
make up
one colour kept for nature

Blue and green
together –
Chung Sun told me this:

And dancing blue lobelias

just now
upon the window-sill

Tip-step me into suddenness
my copper
nerves stripped bare

At sight of sea and land
beyond
the sea and further tumbling sky

Repeated land and sky
and layers
of sea and land and sky again

Unending green all blue
all colours
breath – all movement all

All colours
flow
all colours – all

all movement air
until

all colour
green and blue

Na hEallaí

This is my ship
and the storm outside is you

all of you – and absence
irregular bursts of thunder

again I close the shutters
open them

throw logs on the fire
and wonder at the early dark

Tonight
I must wash the floors

tomorrow strip the bed
turn off the water

in the pipes – pack my bags
and leave again

Five days now I've been
imprisoned

with that ambivalent
pronoun *you* –

that signifies presence
absence silence

do *you* remember
reading to me

for the sick and dying
in the black-bound

Book of
Common Prayer

to comfort me keep me
from drowning

in delirium
being lost in absence

Until now: and the only *you*
I can speak to

is absence is silence
is silence is distance

is absence is distance
is you

Street Scenes: Neighbours

The little birds
is cunts
said my neighbour
is cunts
the little birds
and they eat everything

And I see
they're cutting
the trees in Manders
and I hope they do
them fuckers too

Waving his fist
at the stand of trees
down at the bottom
of my garden

But the little birds
is the hoors

Mind you – he
continues
spotting a neighbour
from five doors down –

There's a queer
lot of cunts
that live around here
when you
come to think about it

Wotan's Feast

for Donald Sur

1.
For fourteen days
the rain
had prowled the yards
in Boston

2.
Inside for the feast
there were
letters and words
to stick on the fridge –
family and
a book on Architecture

crispy-chicken
lobster

smoked salmon
cauliflower

beef bean-curds
broccoli

saumon au gratin
roast-duck

oyster-pancakes
prawns

carrots
asparagus cheese

and a birthday cake
like a curling-stone

3.
outside in the rain
the father and son
I've been seeing all day
speaking English Russian
Greek Haitian
Portuguese –
(obrigado I say *obrigado)*

4.
Would it matter in the end
if there were no candles
no candles there
but there were
or even if you were not there
but you were
for Sefauchi's Farewell
played
in the night
before Aughrim

5.
Donald –
in times of rain
and days and nights
of rain-to-come

letters and words
to stick on the fridge
and a birthday cake
like a curling-stone

The Aspect Of The Russian Verb

for Giuseppe Santarella

The aspect of the verb
I go
depends on if I go on foot
or ride
or with another
take a bus
with a perfect or imperfect end in view

And if I go from here
to there
(perhaps intending first
to travel somewhere else)
my end may be decided in the end
on pure semantics

Giuseppe tells me
that's why Russians shout
shto shto
what what
when asked directions:
needing you to clarify
the aspects
the semantics of the verb:

Astray
in Longford yesterday
a young man with a shotgun
held the police at bay –
a night and day with
shotgun-blasts and music:

He is very agitated
said the tellymen portentously –
we've heard loud music
he's been playing music loud
all afternoon
the volume turned up full:
they do not say
what music he is playing –
what he hears –
nor care
to clarify the aspects of the verb:

The verbs *to be to die*
to love to hear – last night we heard
the young man
and his music both were gone
shot dead
and silent cold
an end to movement
and to music and to verbs:

The lilac's out today
beneath my window –
Niall plays loud music here
he beats the drums
and plays the music loud
all afternoon –
this place being where he lives

within the aspect of the verb
I hope
the lilac blooms for him

April 21st 2000   Niall's Birthday

Immagine Uomini: For Paul Cahill
On His Fiftieth

It was our Sicilian friend
il barbiere di Magione
who told us of one another:
Lei conosce
il Professore Irlandese
con barba rossa?
E conosce lei
Il scrittore Irlandese
con barba nera?

He too is dead now
gone to rest
and the scaffolding is down
from
the tower of the Longobardi
first time
in twenty years
I've seen it naked
bare-faced stone

The twenty years I've seen
the beard
sea-change
from black to grey
iron
in the colour of the lake
iron in the soul and eyes

Roux et noir
it comes to this –

our personal
acquaintance with mythologies:
across the road
from my new-barbered head
just now –
I'm walking home –
I see the same three aged men
in shade
beside the refuse bins
upon the same three
ancient seats

Beneath the skin
three fates
measuring out the thread
by knots:
for generations
playing cards
discussing time and place

from The Nightingale Water

Evening Light

In silhouette
against
the evening light
a figure locked
in a private myth

sitting up
in bed
pushing the rocks
of time
from your knees

a warm south
wind
blows in today
from the sea
and oh just once

to see you lying
back or
lying down to sleep
just that –
to be done

with the task
of giving up –
I'd wish you absent
to be gone
from this

to be taking your ease
ag ligint do scíth
in feathers
of ducks
like Eibhlín Dubh

not tantalised
at the end so
pushing shards
of hope and faith
around a bed

Mrs Pike

Mrs Pike
the woman breathing
in the next bed
died today
at seven in the morning –
on her 90th birthday
plus a day
God rest her

there are too many
poems
in this twilight place –

The woman
in that bed tonight
whose name
I shall learn
asked me after she
dropped her glass –
who owns
that big dog?

Second Night-Stroke

The force of
gravity
that struck again
on wings
of blood
swooped upward
to the brain

hit random
home
and terrible
again:
turned round and round
and struck
again:

the purposeful
assassin
locked into
the genes
to flesh the circle out:

hits home
in the extended
time
of night
stretched thin
to find us

trusting
open
naked or asleep

July Twelfth

I woke this
morning
after three hours sleep
to hear the news
and felt the breath
of evil
in my house

In
Ballymoney
in the night
three children
firebombed
burnt to death:

the Devil walked
abroad
among the drums
and preachers'
talk

incited madmen
in the blood
and dark
this hateful week
of rhetoric
to leave
a dirty smoke-stained wall
his monument:
three children
inside
burnt to death

and what can I do
but name them
say
their names again
for meaning:

Richard
Mark and
Jason Quinn

that they were here
as we
identical
and various

may
this preserve us
at the end

      this day
and all our days
from giving up on hope
from giving in
to weariness
despair and weariness

from failing life
through weariness

XXIII

I thought of Jack
again
                    that poem
Urlár soimint
                    aige ag rinnce

        the cement floor
                    and you wouldn't
have a stitch
of a shoe on you after:

                    and show me that ...
                    pullover
                    I used to put buttons
                    like that
        and the lace
on Siabhra's socks:

        and that's the shawl
        that Redwan's mother sent
        from Libya
... it was good
of her:
last thing
tonight before we leave

we ask the nurses
for a note

to take us quickly through
tomorrow's cordon
around the cyclists
of the Tour de France

Small Hours

Things we forget
to record
lost like
all the songs
and poems
in one head

things reminding us
of themselves

record me
record me
write me down

the horse I hear
each night
I lie awake

lonely
hoof-beats
in the Ranelagh Road

Riddle

Today
on
St Mac Dara's Day
a changed
dimension
there is
an absence

some other
doorway opening

a road
I do not know

… as I came over
a windy gap
I met my Uncle Davy

The place
we occupy –
in you
I recognise the tilt
and setting
of the shoulders:
the family

not one of them
could die in peace

… I laid him down
and sucked his blood
and left his body aisy

walking the land
a preparation

in the stance
and in the head

Hiatus

In this pre-thunder
yellow light

before the summer storm
I see my mother

now in effigy asleep
at last

imperious
head thrown back

a Pharaoh
in a poem of mine

from twenty years
and more ago:

strange how things
come home

come back come round
again –

those Egyptians in the
X-ray pictures

yellow hair
combed back from brow

the sea-girl
out of Keegan's fish shop

saved once again by
Ruggiero

or the Norman knight
on catafalque

I saw
that day in Vezelay

these skip
the circuits of the brain

redraw
the rules of memory:

And someone else
will come in time

to scan
these dreadful months

our crooked span of pain
and doubt

reliving
how they fell in love got drunk

or made love on a summer
night

saw the past come round
again

or saw their
children's children born

Roles

We have all
become

like children
in the park

when I was
young

who played
a game

of then you
must

and then
I must

and then you
must

and now
the nurses say

they read
my Whitsun

poem to you
at night

to ease
the agitation

sometimes
in the

small hours
two a.m.

Mindscapes

          You dreamt
you were left in a field
all night
in a shed in a field
a bothán
on the Old McConnells'
land:
          the ones who hid
the half-moon parings
of their nails
and their folded locks
of hair
in hollow places
in the walls:
          but which of us
wouldn't
prefer to lie out
in a field at night
to be gone from here
and wake with leaves
about the bed
          recalling mysteries
the old Road
underneath a ditch
the line
between the farms
a rough-flagged path
where mushrooms grew
from stones: as I
          remember it
you warn me now

of nettles
stinging plants
and the cure
grows near the cause –

I think of this
and walk
into the sea today
along an
eighteenth century road –
the lines
beneath the earth

the rowan tree
the human heart

the cure
beside the cause

Seeing

Signs that come
on the wind

burrs
and twigs and leaves

the signs your mother
would read

in a dog's coat
there is no cure

for any of this

Us Then

These were not
the sounds of my childhood
of the ornamental singing
this is not how you were

Speaking in tongues
with Madame Maud Gonne
in the Roebuck Palace
of the Quicken Trees

Now they say you ramble
when you name the names –
for the people you call on
are dead and gone

Agus cabbair ni ghairfead féin
something else I've learned –
Dar an leabhar dá ngairinn
níor ghaire-de an ti dhomhsa

But you and I forever
in the snows of forty-seven
making our way
to the number Eight tram

And didn't we take pride
in the Old Road to Tara
that crossed our parcel
of no-man's-land

Your Mother

The last time your mother
my grandmother
walked into Athboy
a man working in the plantings
cut her a stick
a cane for her journey
her last:

all her life she had prayed
for three days
warning of death:

a vessel burst in her brain
as she walked
past the wall
of the undertaker's yard:

she died
in a friend's house
36 hours later

in her pocket
two letters

in her glasses-case
money

for Masses: for
the Repose of her Soul

and peace among
her quarreling children

There

From next door
raised
a querulous angry
old woman's voice

"... Cow Cow
What are you saying
cow for?

There's no cows here
unless you're the cow

And I know what kind
of cow you are ..."

This

This is what people do
cry out
go on journeys in the night

Let me go now
and it'll be
my last caprice

and do you know
what I would love

is water from the well

what I would love
to have
is some of that
nice
nightingale water

I write it down
as writers do

do texts destroy each other
and themselves?

We

We are the whisperers in
the shadows
we talk of times-past signposts
the Granard Bus
Joe Duffy radio programmes
the present scandals
brown paper bags and envelopes
stuffed with cash –
fifty grand the going rate
for an item of chicanery
a hundred and eighty thousand
to keep the Celtic Helicopter
flying …

This is the kind of stuff
we mention
rehearse in whispers
while we wait
keep vigil and wait
for a change in the breathing
and that's the kind of affair
it is in the end
after all the shouting and roaring
the bravado and the baroque
to be getting ready
like swallows on the
telegraph wires in Autumn

Frowning a little
before the plunge
to open the wings and off

from Artichoke Wine

Here In The Darkness

Here in the darkness
alone beyond talk
I talk to myself
where the talking stops

World's drying up
world's gone grey
now the rain falls down
through the hole in May

Alone in the darkness
inside my eyes
walking through fields
and mackerel skies

Tomorrow I'm going
tomorrow I'll be gone
see my doctor first
get fixed up if I can

I'm taking a boat
sailing far far away
nothing was promised
and nothing was paid

Here in the darkness
alone beyond talk
I talk for myself
when the talking stops

Here in the darkness
biding my time
with memories of sunlight
and artichoke wine

West Going West

Walking down O'Curry Street
and looking at Egan's Marble Bar
... is this where it was... Kilkee
where we danced in the sea
in winter...
myself Gail Price and Michael Hartnett
before being run out of town
by the Sergeant
more than their several lives ago
and to think *like exclusion*
we might have made it important:

This man I hire the bike from
could he have heard the story?
Or the present staff
of the Bank Of Ireland
where they cashed me a cheque for a fiver
drawn on trust
identity being the poem I recited
while word by word they followed the text

Best part of forty years ago:
and my benefactor
John McCarter
has long since joined the martyrs
in Letterkenny of the traffic lights
prophesied by Columcille:

And I cannot get back to today
the starting-point of itself
till I stop
for bread and milk in Carrigaholt:

You're a writer then –
you write yourself?
I'm quizzed by the man in the shop
Do you know James Liddy?
Or Brendan Kennelly?

On my long trip West
on this stony road
I keep my counsel still
on falling foul of the beatitudes –
and... the loneliness...
of their rejection –
for dancing in the sea one winter here
before
being run out of town by the Guards:

surviving
the same crooked passing of time
and the strange imperfect Masonry of poets

Raskolnikov

Coming home from Rathmines
I notice
The ladders and buckets and tins of paint still there
In a house I worked in once

This kind of noticing began
One summer I passed
The nineteen sixties concrete block
Where I navvied in Hyde Park Lane

Now grown old and stained
And tacky and dull:
But of all the half finished rooms that wait
For something in the afternoon

Clearest of all
Was in St Petersburg – when I looked
Across the canal
As the bells rang out above

At that particular house:
The ladders and buckets and tins of paint still there
The murder that hasn't happened yet
And the student pausing on the stairs

Casas Colgadas

It was the great blind backs of the houses
I loved as a child
the high-up returns
and cabinets and superstructures
fumbling from the cliff
like the casas colgadas in Cuenca –
where I never managed
to spend that winter
warmed by burning wood
and *Fundador* yet staying austere
in the cold monastic picture I'd invented
for making poems –

It was the great blind backs
of the Dublin houses I loved then
and still love now
and how on sunlit mornings
or sunny slanting afternoons
they can surprise you:
all the random muffled shapes
in the wrapping
that pushing bulging strangeness
underneath the skin

At Selles-Sur-Cher: August 22nd 2001

Awake tonight again
I have become
that drawing
in the house in Dublin ...
hospital patient
chalk on paper Paddy Graham
nineteen seventy-four
in old red-striped pyjama jacket
crouched on an iron bed
locked in The Mental
and world in his head
hand to face he stares at me
has stared for years
cheekbone and jawbone
bludgeoned by time

In this hotel room now
woken from sleep
and more than past my half-way point
in the middle of the night I crouch
alone on the edge of the bed
hunched up like him
in unforgiving neon light
searching in the corners
for how and why:

Even the notes I made
In the back of the book
Have fallen apart

Won't work – will not reform
For memory or reading glass

In the end and only
the outside sound of the trains
connects – the trains
that sweep through midland towns
to pick us up and drop us down
in random rooms
at random points
with our luggage of clocks and charts
and sticks of chalk
for making marks:

the tracks in the air connect
reach out
from the painted hand on the wall of the cave
reach out
from here to the ends of the earth

Green November: Missiano 2001

Last time I walked this bit of road
like this
was Easter five years back
and the Grannies were out
let out after winter
and then

Up the hill with them
shawls flying in the wind
rocketing on sticks
pointing out who lived where
and when – locating all
the marks upon the landscape
yet again:

This little stretch
between the graveyards
the Via Gramsci
taking over
from the Via Sant' Urbano:

Today like then
is beautiful and clean
so focussed clear the air
is like a lens imprinting me
among the hills
and hidden things

As when I leave this road
to come down into Africa
across the fields

that patch I know
of cracked bare winter earth
scratched with the tracks of beasts
recorded time
in muddy prints

Or the man below
who stops hand up
blue coat flapping in the wind
to look at me
shading his eyes from the sun

Or the tall thin shepherd yesterday
beside my house
black beard and crook
who grazed his sheep
just passing by – so quick
no more than half an hour
in the small green fields
on each side of the road

But while it happened
all this little piece
of countryside was full
was loud with bells
the clatter and clang of sheep
and then filled up with absence after
music ended
they were gone

And like this last white rose
so white
above my yard
high up beside the gable-light

Cigne: At Sixty

for Tony MacMahon

A man goes by beneath the window
a tank of poison on his back
to spray the vines

Sinews and signals
in my arm
roots and cables in the ground

And I'm listening
alone in the sun-baked yard
to the dancing march

MacMahon from Clare
playing *The Haughs of Cromdale*
to a row of butchered trees

Hacked and lopped
in the wake
of the ENEL Maintainance/Repair

And I cried:
for all of us over and over I cried
in the shadowless sun

And I don't know yet
what it meant or not
beyond that I found myself crying

Alone in the full of the sun at sixty
for I suddenly knew
there had never been any road else but this

To *The Haughs of Cromdale*
in the sun
and the battered stumps of trees

Richard Riordan Leaving Glenaulin

Dear Dickie –
As you said yourself of Robert MacBryde
you were very quick to be gone in the end
on an August evening
in Chapelizod by smooth river water
      by the weir
where Adrian joked you looked so butch
last Christmas in my leather jacket

(in the Korean poem
the busy flowers of a river village
are best seen from afar)

And I think of you at the end
setting out from your bed-side shrine
of the Virgin Mother and Michelangelo's David
though not for Santiago:

For an old Kavafy hand like you
(the vigil among flowers
of silence
      the beautiful young Filipina nurses
bright-eyed women
      voiced like birds)
to die among the beautiful young
is almost right
      for letting go

To engage with MacBryde's Venusians
so beautiful he said –
like Rilke's angel

271

who sees no line between the living and the dead –
you wouldn't know if they were girls or boys

Or busy flowers or voices from the weir –
or in Tangiers
the young men on the beach –
but life's so short
so little time
despite the seeming permanence of things

The permanence of sixty passing years at large
an autumn garden in the sun
the dip of water over stone
Too short Too short
one afternoon is too much like another
even with the voices-off
and marvellous figures in the mind

Until this trial we make of letting go
(and they tell me
          it was hard for you – how could it not –
the shutting down
the body letting go of life
old lover loosing the clutch of love)

the journey without shoes or staff or hat or shells
out there by Séipéal Iseult and beyond

That December

Am I too late I asked
to be remade
been too long there
at the back of the grate
too many times
reduced by flame?

Today a message
from the clinkers of my past:
North Africa
by hand: the last day of the year

A man in Libya
telling it
over and over again:
> *the sun*
> *behind the sun*
> *behind the sun*
> *behind the sun*

If I go on saying this
he says
no one can take me
> from myself

How It Is

1.
Aloysius Bertrand
dying in the Hôpital
Necker
in 1841
still worried about
the state of his manuscript

No family member
attended the interment

His sister
preparing herself for marriage
had arranged
that afternoon
to try out a new piano

2.
Those Kenyan dancers
blown to bits
by the bombers
in the Paradise Hotel:

When the families came
to collect them
to gather them home
to the waiting graves

The hospital held
the bits of bodies in pawn

till someone could pay
the mortuary bill

3.
Mehr licht mehr licht
as Goethe said
at the end
mehr licht more light
and more light getting through
until at last
we become unseen

In The Ranelagh Gardens, September 2002

for Ben Dwyer

NONE

No means beyond:
and I'm falling
as I told you

Nietzsche throwing his arms
about the horse
in the street

Collapsed into madness
and it's all
too late

A *fait accompli*
only
I don't have the means to hand

The well-greased click
and tincture of oil
and smoke

The blow to the head
and the broken
egg in the grass

VOICES

Death changes the appointment
time and place:
and so do I

That stranger
in my body – a dizziness
that comes and goes

Next time I see her
I am walking
in the park

Rats swim
and she is young and thin
and inarticulate

Dressed up in silver gauze
to lend some weight
to what she says

The voices…oh I can't explain
she starts again
and flaps her arms:

When I look up
into the moon I think
that that's my home

My own two hands wiped clean
I light a light
inside a room inside a room

FATHERS

A weak man? No –
unroofed I think
and open to the skies

Unable for our common lot
of pity:
the fiercely broken heart

Of sharing this
of walking down the
city street

And not being blind –
at home
he sat inside the dark

Is with me still –
I saw a child today
with half a face

A sudden slip
of reason in the street
a half-man in the park

In front of me
a woman
who had wet herself

I bring the image
home – it's all I know
of what we do:

For fear that children
going to school
might see

Each night
we sweep the blood up
from the path

Contact

There is no body contact here
no touch
and that's the trick

Like city traffic –
an accident
that doesn't happen

We move into the space
where someone else
has been

Except for
Can we take a moment of your time
when two young mormons

Hail me
full of bonhomie
and teeth

And suddenly the morning
turns around
falls into place

It is not good
to bring up children
looking out through gates

FOOLS

He wanders daily
in the park –
a thin dishevelment

With red moustache
red sun-burnt skin
and floating eyes

Can in hand
he tries to talk
to all the scattered limbs

I am a man – a man
and this is not New York
he says not yet

I want to tell them but
they only want to lie there
in the sun

I'm going to swim
but not in there –
he steps back from the pond

I try to tell them but they
walk away
don't want to know

There is no sun:
the sun has gone
in Dublin and New York

ACCESS

The park again on Sunday
afternoon:
father and infant daughter

Beside the pond
in weekend access time
estranged not quite at ease

And three boys fishing –
Daddy
is that deep in there?

Deep green water
tunnelled by shadows
of fish

Too deep for Daddy
too deep
for Sunday access afternoons

Where is he? Where?
There? Where? Oh there...
and suddenly he sees it now

Their lifeline
stretching off along
these narrow mapped-out paths:

Old grey-fish carp
in shadow
changes into stone

HERON

Sit here and look
how everything is
once repeated

A heron
standing in the rushes
lozenge body

A lifetime spent as
man and bird
globule shape

Of water-light
reflected
from his underside

He fills
the undistracted silence
of himself

The empty park
the little breeze across
the lake

And silence:
in his own dimension
of bird and fish

And bird alone
to be
as different as that

GODS

Three young boys
fishing –
in the afternoon

Grown bored
with ritual
decide on

Trawling the barbs
across the pond
to hook

A golden belly
or back
with one quick jerk

Drag out
some grey-backed
shadow

Of wind and bird
to drown
in the burning air

Keep him out
he jumped – he jumped
he's still alive

Keep him out
till I have a look –
poor random fish

Poor straining
useless gasp
of golden breath

MYTHOLOGY

The schoolgirl
outside in the street just now
the same

As that
old woman
watching from the trees

I recognise them both
all fractured images
repeated

The lizard overlay
of truth and lies
and how

A young girl
laughing in the street
just now

Is here
an ancient woman looking out
between the leaves

JUDGEMENT

And in the end
who cares who lies down
naked here

Outside of death
who really lies down naked
any more...

When you are
young
you own the world

And this is how
the world
unfolds – this search for sense

And shape:
all else
has passed me by

Upon these paths
my eyes half-shut against
the glare

Of reassembling flesh:
these
broken painted parts

IDENTITY

Cold and wet
she sat here
crying in the rain –

*I don't know where
I'm from
she said – or how*

*Is there a hospital
near here
somewhere nearby*

*That's where
I started out today
someplace*

*I don't know where
I am
or who was there*

*Out there it was
somewhere
out there today*

*This morning yes…
and
I was there…*

*Today:
the mountains maybe
or the sea*

LOCKSMITH

Arcane signs
are cut into the archway
of the gate

And here
the nuns would pass out
tailored shrouds

Before they too
closed up the business deal
moved on

The park remains:
the Harcourt Railway Line
is reinstated

My neighbours
have declared themselves apart
behind electric gates

It comes and goes
we all are prisoners of the heart
at base

My poem is when
the tumblers in the lock fall
into place

The Cello Suites

1.
Not where it begins at all
but where I come in….
feeling the clarity:
the kettle
a Brâncuşi head
shining convex:
glittering
blue-flame teeth below

I see better
in the house of silence –
Goya's Quinta del Sordo
heartbreak
for those who can hear

I cried when I heard
The New Orleans Band
dancing along
the Corso Vanucci –

Marie Laveau the voodoo queen:
snaps her fingers
shakes her head:
tells about your lovers
living and dead…

289

2.
how my hand
closes around
this fitful sleep
stone
physical
remembering
a humming bird:
a little Chinese knife
all this month
in my hand
as I slept
a little Chinese knife

3.
Cock-crow in June
the starting of the dawn

"....toujours Marrakshi"
as the waiter said

outside the early-morning café
in Gueliz:

I think of London's Forte-light
Good Catholic Firm

Said the mad old nun:
till we got out from giving thanks

Kick-start of a motor-bike
with Rustum Framrose doing ninety

From Marble Arch
through sleeping England

In flight from marking time
the flowing now:

To light down here in Umbria
a lifetime later

Watching the fowl
in the neighbour's haggard

Cry out into the mixing dark
and morning light

The dilute mist – I clear a space
to make a start

4.
I hear + my father's + voice…
again…
and + I am
following + that voice + the ghost

5.
I caught a glimpse of wings
today in the yard
above the ruined trees
An Buachailín Bán Lament for the Books
this is the long hard road they said
and I'm the old dog at the end

To the *Haughs of Cromdale*
I danced on my doorstep
dancing alone and wanting a drink
all that I remember
and the long-feathered birds
gathered for the feast

6.
Flutter of wings
at the back
of the polished box

feather and fear
and I hear the varnished sounds
down deep

1.
Driving over the country road
to La Goga in November
on the back-route under Agello
with my heart breaking
I found myself saying
we were happy here
we were happy here
Is this how we remember things?

The French woman
looking round the yard
with tears in her eyes
the day the house changed hands
saying in a broken voice
we were happy here
we were happy here
Is this how we remember things?

2.
Eiléan and Niall
and the fog-farm
where the mist grows:
to recall it hurts me

3.
It is all desire:
that house up there
on the flat-topped hill
buttressed pubic mound

juts out
and the dry land
of the valley
beats like waves
upon the slopes beneath:

this inland place
was always sea –
and pinned up on a gate
today I find a notice
still intact
but faded from the sun:

sei come il mare
ed ogni onda
e il battito del mio cuore

4.
When Eilís was ill
the ear they said
is the last to go –
play for her now
those sounds she liked to hear
and you did
through the terrible Spring

It was
the shaded place in Córdoba
an envelope of sound
in Leeson Park
inside a room

In her house I remember
the cello
that stood in the hall – cool
container of sound
sober and curved and beautiful
silent in the corner
as if it were

As if those curves
shaped conch and scroll
could ever be silent
even at rest:
as my mother too who was deaf
but sang all her life

5.
In spite of supercilious Latham:
she did:
"A drawing
made by Mrs Blake
taken from something
she saw in the fire
during her residence with me.
Curious as by her"

6.
Father I have been
listening to music
to music like darkness
all interior:

I heard the Chinese poet
Duo Duo
reading his poems aloud:

This is how it was
I thought
is who you were:

A water ghost
beside some eastern river

COURANTE

1.
I crossed Ireland in the rain
last week of May
to see Anne Donnelly's paintings
heads islands birds –

Stopped the music a moment
at Lough Owel
great stretch of water for a Meath man
my childhood inland sea

And I thought of my Uncle James
how he stepped over
opened land
an apron of seed strapped round his waist
the mantra was all
in the sweep of his arm
the grains he scattered from his finger tips:
history centered about himself

2.
Three swans flown in from Moyle
all coloured now
by this dark sound
dark as the brown bog-water

3.
The fiddler in the cave
holds back the sea:
the firbolgs planted the land like this

the smoky kitchen
candle-light
on mother of pearl:

This side of the doorway
let me feel it
let me put
my hand there let me
hold it
touch it
feel it

let me somehow stay connected

4.
I'm drifting further
even here
in the main piazza
anchored to the Bar Gallo –

Over the surface of the lake
over the heads of men
standing round talking
smoking and chatting
on Sunday morning:

Above the Uncles
their backs against Tom Murphy's window
after Mass
in Athboy on a Sunday
Stouts and Ales
And Whiskey Bonder

And I'm floating over us all
on music and fever
of hair on string
time and the moon
and myself
and the native generations buried here
like horses' skulls
beneath the hearth

5.
Stripped as bare as
Saint Sebastian
not here at all
with my ears blocked
I think of the child
born too soon
locked in a room
forbidden to talk
the moral choice
of the beaten poor
the present being present
by fear of fear…
stripped as bare
as this naked man
afraid to start
such remembering

6.
I am unpeeling as the skin unpeels
in the Anatomy Class
in the varnished room:
how many hundred students carved their names

in the grooved wood?
I feel the touch of strings across my skin:
like Marsyas
poor Satyr
flayed for making music

Where are you now?
At night
Hoof-beat footfall from the yard
Hoof stamp my remembering....

SARABANDE

1.
This is
the apparatus of the usual

In the cathedral
Et spes nostra salve

The idea
more than the thing itself

Seashore smell
of August silage

Embracing all
the queer and broken

In this fourth Prélude
over and over

It is the bell sound
in the wood

2.
The engine room of Brunel's *Great Britain*
Is the true Turbine of the Tate Modern

3.
Marsyas exhibited
pinned out
the inner dark displayed –

Kapoor's great curved red sky
red membrane
stretching over our heads
and beyond
a phonograph swoop
repeated
over and over
vibrating firmament of skin:
dordán
red dry drone of bees in the afternoon
red noise behind the eyes

as a torch in a darkened room
shines through the fingers
lighting up
the warm blood of the hand

the sea beneath
the abattoir at Algeciras ....

4.
We are not looking up
into the sky
at all
but into sheets and halliards:

It is an afternoon of thunder
a summer storm
a terrible electric sky
in Germany

It is Brunel's Great Boat
pushing through the Atlantic

deck vernissage
humming beneath our feet

It is the icy salt
that breaks
across
the sea-wall

And we are looking up
beyond the sky
past blood and bone
and tissue

Into the inner place
beyond the ear
within the dark
inside of things

5.
A child I saw the body of a sheep
that had been gored
and partly flayed:
the green hole inside the skin
is where the horn went in

6.
Our childhoods
all raked-up

the old road underneath the ditch
old wheel-ruts on the path

Houses we don't go back to
stopping at the gates

Under these flagstones
this paving
in the square
under all these layers of people
built into these Mayan houses
in the hollow walls
and basements
who lies where?

BOUREÉ

1.
From Busáras
the Derry bus swings out
past the Coroner's Court
the lizard sits in the sun alert:
beneath the hearth
the horse's head vibrates
reverberations of things
we heard as children –
poor mad pachyderm
Madre de Noche Oscura
I am the Elephant up in the Zoo
as she threw
great tumbling blocks of furniture
around the childhood room

2.
Have I dealt with that:
in the *Quinta del Sordo*
the Deaf Man's House
it is the silence that brings me back –
the silent bushes
flying past my window
the pilgrimage of San Isidro
the gaptooth silent notes

3.
Unter den Linden
it is what isn't there

The past being present
by absence

In Berlin East
the Ishtar Gate of Babylon:

A blood-red dress...
Potzdammer Platz

Red scarf... the Bank of Ireland
steps

The same
you think with

Only 40 years of time
between

But being here
the moment we are in

Is where
the straight lines meet –

The Terraced House
that isn't there

The space
of missing books:

In Koppenplatz
bronze table upturned chair

4.
The pleasure boats sail by beneath
and you – she said –
are you ever...carefree...
I don't even know what the question means

....*aber ich habe sie verloren*
and not just you but time

alone I slept in satin sheets
alone I learned her City streets

and the name of the riverboat below
was *Nostalgie Berlin*

5.
Stumbling in the desert sun
the blinded dinosaur swings round
directed onward
by the brain inside its tail

the stranger in my body
yes
the bird that flew before me on the path

6.
Water always
slopped from the bucket
on the way home from the well:

The Faustian Bargain
clear at last
in a Viennese Café:

The hollow horseman
on the road to Sligo
outlined on a hill

The stars
above the Prater Luna Park
Rotha Mór an tSaoil
the roadsign for Budapest
the motionless Big Wheel

GIGUE

1.
In Derry
one man at one
with the beautiful seahorse creatures
controls the room –
the strings that hold us here
his countless hours
of playing this
until the imprint is
laid down
beneath the skin
the present where the strings meet
nunc fluens
and *nunc stans:*

Contagion of healing
…hard knowledge
where the horns went in

2.
Energy freed from wood and bone
From air
The atoms of sound

Flow up between his hands
Like water
From a sudden spring

A flame that slips
From log to log
Fills up the shell of time

3.
Black feathers
and tassels
on his long black coat

Agent + artificer + adept
Soundholder
Boxboat
Iceflower
Birdsoul
Goatneck
Horsedrum
Resinate
Woodvoice
Barrowtongue

One road only in the end

That's where he'd be
down there
practicing his dancing
on the rocks

4.
Shaman or Satyr
or Father of the Church

Marsyas flayed
for making true music

Victim
to mystification

The King of Judges
had Ass's lugs

5.
In the empty Sacristy
Of the Cathedral
The fine oak table
And heavy chairs

Where the City Fathers
Held council
Through the long days
Of the siege

With the Unthinkable
Outside the walls
A stone's throw
From their windows:

History as fact
The myth of opinion
And language only
The lie to believe in:

6.
Light changes:
the northern room grows dark still resonating

In the walled city
beneath the Army Post

Last winter here
a handful of gravel thrown at the soldiers

Quick scatter of noise
a rattle of stones like frost

Tavernelle di Panicale, July 2003

Driving To Charleston

The "Noise" You Hear
Is The Sound Of Freedom –

Chiselled letters
cut into the wall
of the Marine Base
in Beaufort South Carolina
the day we drove to Charleston –
I wanted to see Fort Sumter
and the US Army
was making for Baghdad –
the beautiful black girl
in the filling-station
a flower of the forest
in a bright yellow singlet
whose every cell was a hymn to life

Bomb em all she said
crossing the forecourt
Bomb em all
                    and bring
Our boys back home.

In the Low Country
            just to the north of the Gullah people
with palmettos
prayer houses
African fish-nets spread in the shade and indigo Batik
a sea-road back
to Sierra Leone

Terrible to see
the Stalinist slogans
blowing in on the wind like spores
from the edge of the mind
and finding root:

The night before
at the Junior Chamber of Commerce Awards
when Billy Bob gave thanks
in the name of Christ
and our boys who serve overseas
so that we may continue
to have meals like this

The man on my right
Marine Captain
in full Dress Uniform

He'd been there before
in Desert Storm...
for him it was *deja vue*
he said
And how do they feel in Europe
about the Action?
His own parents were Portuguese
and of course they supported the war

But I hear there's people
over there
who don't get to see American TV
and don't know what's going on...
and of course when...
when...those Lefts
                    get into it....

Well… there's a time and a place…
there's a time and a place:

And those guys now
will get twice as many medals as these:

Triumphal voice of Fox avant la lettre
and a year later
I'm looking at the sad pictures
of Lynndie England
holding a naked Iraqi on a leash
and her grinning lover
in bright-green latex gloves
arms folded
behind a pyramid of naked prisoners

Specialist Charles Graner
who had "a history of troubles"

Looking at them and thinking
of that young woman on the way to Charleston
so beautiful
my breath stopped –
                    Bomb em all
                    Bomb em all
And bring our boys back home

And thinking of Jessica Lynch
whose story was stolen
after she was saved   traduced
and taken away
to be turned into myth:

In fraud we trust
when truth is lost

2.
Said Colleen Kesner   from Fort Ashby:

To the country boys here
if you're
a different nationality   a different race
you're subhuman
that's the way girls   like Lynndie were raised

Tormenting Iraqis
would be no different   from shooting a turkey

3.
And at least you can come
to grips with that
but where was the threat
for New York
in the six months pregnant
Crystal Rivera
fined fifty dollars
for taking a breather
on the subway stairs

Pedro Nazario
aged eighty six
fined for feeding pigeons
in Manhattan

Or the man in the Bronx
who was fined
for sitting on a milk-crate

The man in Staten Island
fined

because the print on his car-inspection ticket
faded

The sleepy tourist
in the subway train
who nodded off   leaned sideways
and was fined
for taking up two seats

Or the woman in Manhattan
fined for using
the wrong-coloured
garbage recycling bags

4.
You're either with us
Or you're with the terrorists

5.
Let me try to tell you where I've been:

reading poems in Cambridge
and in South Boston
remembering Korean friends

walking the sociable streets
in Manhattan
at Pat Kaufman's direction

watching the elephant seals
colonise the marina
in San Francisco

lost in the living heartbeat silence
of Serpent Mound
near Cincinnati

listening to *lieder*
sung in the Union Street Bar
at midnight in Detroit

seduced by blues-man Sugar Blue
and Caravaggio's camp angel
in Chicago

on a long white road
in the Ozarks
drowning in dog-wood and blood-red birds

in a picture frame in
winter sunset
looking down on the upper Hudson

driving the backroads of Appalachia
with Bill Williams
following the Ohio river

travelling twenty-four hours
on a train
from West Palm Beach to New York

celebrating the Wright Brothers
in a bookstore
in a cloudburst in Dayton Ohio

with Thomas Lynch
hunting for an old-style soda fountain
on the road to Kalamazoo

journeying round Saint Louis
for days
in search of Wingfields

in the Civil War cemetery
with the dead of North and South
in Fayetteville

having hominy grits
eggs bacon gravy and biscuits
for breakfast

in a Club Car on a train
listening to the Canterbury Tales
take place around me

reading poems for hours
unplanned
in an Irish bar in Trenton New Jersey

watching the moon come up
over the Black Shamrock
in Milwaukee

on Brighton Beach with Pat
in a Russian bistro
eating pelmeniye and borsht

at sea with Sabra Loomis
in the Isabella Gardner House
in Boston

listening to Bach
in a red-brick church
and reading poems in Harrisville

returning to a place of light
suspended
between Prince and Houston

watching the fairy-tale skaters
in Rockefeller Plaza
at midnight

and standing in the snow with respect
in the space
where the Twin Towers stood

6.
May comes and I'm setting out again
for Boston and Toronto
setting out with *The Cello Suites*
and the memory of that Armenian blanket
wrapped around me
when you took us in
the night we were caught in the snow in Keene

Despite the bomber jacket
on the flight-deck
time is the universal gift
April mud is August dust
hunger will come through a hole in the wall
all we are is the movement of peoples
the word was here before the book

And I'm reaching back to the start
to the child at the bottom of the well
to myself
to the man in Manhattan feeding the pigeons

to the sleepy tourist in the subway train
to fish-nets spread in indigo shade
to the Flower of the Forest on the road to Charleston

May / August 2004

The Cormorants

Someone invited them in
and they sat
perched on the backs of chairs
on the mantel
on the banisters and landings
hunched like dowagers
or the terrible mad old man on a horse
I saw one winter
hunting over the fields
near Oxford:

And they took up residence
settled into
our living space
watching us out of their alien eyes
arranging their feathers
to look like fur
a tang of salt and diesel
in the air
as they hopped from room to room
heads cocked
picking up scraps
of household talk:

All that winter
their hooded shapes
absorbed the daylight
shrouded
like statues in Lenten Churches
they were large
full bodied

unyielding oily and plump
if you bumped against them
on the stairs in the dark:

And the house filled up
with the weight
of moisture in the atmosphere
mould grew on the phone
and nobody answered
when we rang
the neighbours couldn't remember
our names:

Everything heavy
with forgetfulness
but for the birds
forever diving
through gaps in the conversation
bringing up words
that had slipped from the page
and colours that slid
off the wall
to fall through the cracks in the floor
or come to rest
with the spoons and forks
in the kitchen drawers:

Till again it was spring
and suddenly
some of the gobbets of thought
the birds dredged up
took shape
on the kitchen floor
where the sun shines in

twisting around until
the birds were named –
our own familiar selves
identified too late:

In the drawer of the desk
the family
of knives and forks
and spoons and spools
of words and thread
and paper bags
and broken things
were meaningless:
were what they were
the soul's detritus
oil-stains on the water
a raft from the Medusa

Houdini's Receipt

Loosening the chains is easy
even down in the dark
but then there's the canvas sack
and the bolted metal box
locked from the outside
and when you're through the box
and the air's running out
there are still the fathoms of water
and the surface ice
and when you break through that
you find it's been raining for weeks

At this point those who know
breathe full and deep
in the welcoming lean of the sea
and walk out of the waves
across the curve of the beach
to make for home –
to make a fire in a hearth swept clean
ash outside
in a galvanised bucket

Kavanagh In Umbria

I have seen him here in November
going home through the dark
on the tractor
a piece of sacking
thrown across his shoulders
against the winter fog
hunched up
between the unseeing olives
and the leafless sticks of vines
marvellously translated
but not translated at all
from where he is:
broken fields perishing calves
November haggard
and the mist where Genesis begins

August 2004

From The April Roads Of Longford

I've been hearing
the marvellous names:
bloodworm butterwort
sphagnum moss –

Been remembering a child
filling up bottles
to hear the sounds –
in the stream
at the end of my grandmother's haggard:

The *bop-bop-bop-bop-bop*
on a rising scale
air and water trading places –
colours of sound and glass
and each one different:

I feel the water and mud
and rising warmth
the flowing puddle
we called a river
me crouched in colour and sound:

And that's what April said –
wherever it is
that far off place
that keeps us here:
how we keep going back to where we are

Aughnagarron School: 28 April 2005

for Donna Marie Mahon and all the others...

What did the wind hear
as it came across the valley
an ear cocked to Aughnagarron?
The mighty music
of five tin whistles
a harp two drums and a fiddle
and in the next room
twenty children
filling the space with dance

Coffee At The Café Rimbaud

The year of the war with Argentina
Thatcher sinking the Belgrano
Her good eye on the election
When I was still in the badlands
And fairly new to Umbria
One morning over in Magione
While Eiléan was buying groceries
I strolled inside my usual bar
For a couple of litres of beer
And a smoke – the ritual putting to rights
After the previous night
And I'm watching the big new
Colour TV in the corner
And there's Mrs Thatcher high domed
Metal curls declaiming
Down her barricaded nose
That we are right and we will do
What has to be done and what we've done
Was right and had to be done
Because we had to do it
And the Falklands are Ours
British as Yorkshire or Tunbridge Wells
As British as the North of Ireland
Or the South of Ireland if it comes to that
To be told what's what
And when and by whom meaning herself
Out and Out and Out – and we will sink
A hundred more Belgranos if we must
Whether sailing out of the zone or not
And I am taking the whole thing in
With my beer inhaling in disbelief
When I seem to hear the landlady say

There that's your Prime Minister
Talking there on the television …
And I don't know what she's going to add
From the Argentine-Italian connection
But I'm quick off the mark with
No Signora in my best vernacular
Ah No Signora assuredly no
That person most certainly no is not
Not my Prime Minister no
Nor of any of mine alive or dead
Sono Irlandese io Signora
And Mrs Thatcher is none of that
I abhor the woman and all she stands for
And soon we are into the Irish Question
And one thing leads to another
As one beer leads to another
In glasses that seem to be getting bigger
As the to-and-fro on the television
Is getting steadily hotter
Until in the end Eiléan comes back
And finds we have instituted
A Republic of international friendship
Of anti-Thatcher fellow-feeling
Viva Las … Viva Las … Viva Las Malvinas
But little good it did
Now that I think back on it
For the hundreds of drowned sailors
Or for the soldiers broken and burnt
Among flocks of sheep
On a South Atlantic rock
But I'm glad we got that straight
About Mrs Thatcher the demon grocer
And who she fought the Falklands for
The shits behind the dogs of war
And the truth is that I'd half-forgotten

The whole affair until today
When I found myself back in Magione
With another drummed-up war in progress
Same old lies come round again
Ridden by Bush and Blair
How we did what we did
What had to be done
Inflicting terror shock and awe
And what we've done is done
And right because we did it
And there I am in the self-same bar
In the self-same sleepy street
To find it all moved round a bit
But very little for twenty years
The geography slightly realigned
Under a change of management
More or less as I am myself
With new umbrellas tables chairs
With a brave new name from the new owners
Musicians and poets
And space for music and readings –
Times and genders passing us by
Au cabaret-vert cinq heures du soir
And here I am to my vast surprise
Once more at large in my sixties with
Deréglement de l'Univers
Out of step and stone cold sober
L'Alchimie du verbe
Certified sane in Magione
Drinking coffee in The Café Rimbaud

August 23 2005

Among The Islands: Vanishing Point

That point within the frame
where all lines meet

Today I saw Rathmines town hall
wrapped up in plastic sheeting

Like canvas flapping
under sail

A semaphore
that I am one with Eurydice –

Left underground forever
left behind

Lost figure
in a forty year delusion

Caught here
where all perspectives meet:

And if you see the goddess
on the hillside

Remember me to her:
green oranges

And ice-cold grapes
that travelled home with me

Bore witness
to the truth that I'd been there

A moment in the light
the present tense

Ask her to name the place again
identify the sounds

The islands where we met –
may meet:

Herself of love and ambiguity
she rules the moon

She owns
the morning and the evening stars

The presses and the oil
and water flowing from the rock

Fruit trees on the mountainside
Sheeps' milk and honey

Hers – all hers
the hidden roads across the bogs:

A fragment reached me
here today

And in itself how wonderful
that was

About
the air lit up and full of singing birds

Wood smoke and eagles
the silence of the sea

Among The Islands: Continuance

The old men leaning
on the city wall

Wear
baseball caps against the sun

To look down on the lake and island
see themselves

Their memories of starting out
unmarked

To be nineteen
and walking naked through the pines:

It is the sea-bed island still
I tell myself –

The pomegranates
growing by the roadside

The lazy flies
that drift about the afternoon:

The wisdom of the Sibyl's rock until
suspended

In a room alone in winter
high above

The flowing street
I was in hell for looking down

For watching her
a woman swimming out to sea

White seal shape gliding
far beneath –

The mocking years
passed through the empty room

An empty room without a grate
a space of vacancy

And ice and age
and all that yearning flesh

And overnight
I aged a lifetime in the cave:

Where I have come to now
the fireflies led me here

Unornamented present tense –
I can believe

The thread from Acheron – how
from above

The vines look like the sea:
and being here

Is now – is unrehearsed for now –
is all there is

At dawn
the pheasant in the mist beneath the leaves

The hare
in the long sweet grass

In the simple daily field across
the road

The badger
treading the mountain path

The boar beneath the window
in the dark:

And have I been there
seen the place where I will lie –

Today high overhead
a pair of falcons taking back the sky

Hadewijch

My first thought was Lautrec
La Goulue entering the Moulin Rouge
Those look-at-me high kicks
And dancing off the cross
Of her own crucifixion
And then I thought of all
Those mediaeval women mystics:

Rita of Cascia Colomba of Rieti
Margaret of Cortona Ida of Louvain
Or Ellen of Udine
And the thirty-two stones
That she put in the soles of her shoes
Because I have so often offended God
With my leaping and dancing
Or Joan The Meatless of Norwich…
Who starved themselves
And changed their worlds around
Exchanging bodies with the Lord:

And how when I was young
The image of male nakedness
A man in agony upon a cross
Hung over every bed
But little talk of naked love:

And perhaps she is a hoofer after all
Dancing in the Rue Pigalle
Or calumnied with Liam Lawlor
In a taxi in from Moscow airport –
What shocks is the offence

So many feel such need to take
That they set about inventing it:

After her Eucharistic union
Catherine of Siena wore
Christ's foreskin as a wedding-ring –
In an ecstasy of penance
Angela da Foligno
Vowing eternal chastity
Stripped off all her clothes
Before the crucifix
And offered herself to Christ:

South of Gallarus free of guilt
Between the mountains and the sea
To be there
To be there leaping with life
To be dancing before the cross like this
In the open-air in your pelt

November 3, 2005

Ceangal

for Joe Woods

FIRST....

1.
There is another house
on top of this
I hear them in their basement
overhead:
                    Journal
Intime
of daily life: the constant pouring
from one vessel to another
occasional rush of words
shovel-scrape
door slam
banging in the pipes
The bath or shower past midnight
and the scavenger
                    the beast
who comes in from the railway track
and noses round my attic window
pushing to get in

It was the corncrake that I missed

The absent figures in the print
myself
and all tangential slanting creatures
yes

The fox that hung on the door at night
The witches I prayed come in

2.
Everywhere I've been
I've come from somewhere else
That snatch of Russian song just now
tells me I was never there:
not even on the night
I saw the famous author come on stage
to sing the words himself

head tilted
        like his photograph
                his nostrils flared

Not in those same words
Inside those words
That unique run of notes

It was the corncrake that I missed
the melting snow…

Not to have been invisible

Just that: to be here at the end
to see ourselves
in those same seats we started out in
when they bring the houselights up

SECOND....

1.
Look at it this way:
    I try again
a gate –
beyond it grass
the merest signs of wheel ruts
leading past the tree

which suddenly is where it's wrong
there was a path
here
where the field has taken over

with no suggestion now
of house or avenue
              or energy
A family
with all the shouting and the rows
the business and the madness
and the plans

Worm filter-light
among the memories
          and daffodils
my mother holding out an orange
the first I'd seen
when I was three

in tandem sex and death:

but the dead are all in exile here
on this side of the gate

the savage pond life underneath the hill:

Sad patchy roadside pines
grown whiskery with age

we cannot tell the story
without having to explain...

2.
Winter coming in again
the nights grow dark
cold and shivering

This is not enough for me

*I have a right to say that speak
the truth*

that this is not enough for me

from too much disillusion
my body starts to turn against itself

THIRD....

1.
But picture this:
I have been looking at this iconography
for months
on my right the Saviour Tower
and St Basil's Cathedral
a hundred yards ahead –

Upstairs unseen
the mirror slips
and sea and sky
and everything is underwater:

Lapping over the top
of the mausoleum
up to the bottom of the campanile:
sinking in the middle
the onion-domes
waist deep in ocean

By chance from the top right corner
                              falls
a ray of glass of ice of almost water:
Milton's descent
in the garden at Felpham:
to enter into Blake
by the heel of the foot –

That right moment just
before the door is shut:
before the living island moves
beneath our feet

at the first touch of the fire
and suddenly all is clear

we are silhouetted figures
walking the seaweed cobbles

2.
Coming home again
is simple:
the marvellous Square
two thirty in the morning:
two figures on horseback
cross over before us
matter of fact
moving together

not to have been invisible

past the hotel and the Kremlin walls
down the hill to the river

from The Cotard Dimension to present

Ranelagh Road Revisited

1.
Again I heard the horse
Last week
Again it caught me by surprise
Hoofbeats
On the hard street

A space between the notes
And then
The fading into silence
The silences between the things
That come to mind ...

A single summer voice
One night in 1990
Going home alone
Olé Olé Olé Olé
Reaching
Over the roof-tops
In through my window

2.
This present Monday
There was almost nothing:
Nothing from the roof
No rattling in the attic
Only the hazy separated blurs
Almost a whisper
All night
Of rain on the glass

On Tuesday night
The wind swept in
And filled the space with hugeness

3.

Three times last night
In the small hours
The horse went trotting up the road
Hoofbeats on glass
In the rain

I heard
The summer voices
Underneath my window
Young couples and late-night drinkers
Sitting on the steps
Discoursing
Devouring the eclipse:

The rusty moon
The colour of dried blood

4.

We think
The things we know
Will last forever:

The young woman
In the house next door
To this
Has died today aged thirty-one

For Pearse Hutchinson

The beast of Yucca Flats
Poor beast
Staggering round in circles
Mad as a crab in the sun

And the nightmare *rose lutin*
Poor elf
Working in the dark
On the chests of sleeping dreamers

The last gaunt plastic bags
Snared in the trees
In the rain
Till the coming of Spring

And in the night-time Cities of Light
Obsidian glass –
The dancers
Waiting silent in the streets

Circles

do JM agus PD Portlaoise

The stillness
reminds me of something

*seven wild birds
in a circle*

Scythian kurgans

Dead horsemen
on dead horses
guarding a dead man buried

hunched rider in the middle

Tonnage
of Stonehenge

Stone heads
on Easter Island
telling us where they want to go

*like the birds
constrained*

Newgrange

My grandmother
20 miles away
with the sun at Easter dancing on the ceiling
burial places

Circles
and machines –
circles within circles

turning the handle
to move around the sun

Lake

A natural low terrain
gouged by ice
water flowing

Downstream
deep and clean
free of sediment

Fills in and forms
a wetland
eventually meadow

Eye

Show not tell
its central
pitiless detachment

Black hole
outpouring
constant focus

Shrinks
chews up the universe
consuming it

Snake

for Áinín Ní Bhroin

This is
where we found the skin a snake had shed

and that the destination of all journeys
is astonishment
and touch

to get there in the end

red blood and spit

black feathers in the sun

It is the snake itself that's green
and not the skin

Tavernelle di Panicale

353

Caltagirone

Christmas cribs in all the churches
Flowers on the giant staircase
Wooden spinning-tops for sale
And the winter-light ceramic glaze

Who are these familiar strangers
Who come home to us?
Whispers and children both
Come from so far distant

The wind is blowing the cyclamens
By the Bridge of San Francesco
And the statue of Gualtierra now
Repeating Sicilian Vespers

Aston Quay: January 2008

Look closely at this streetscape
now
to underline it
see it as it is
As it is? for now and not
for *As it is*
as when you see it in your head
Commercial icons

Burn Our Ear Off
where once
the multi-coloured rays
fanned out from *Bovril*
into the sky
above the Ballast Office

Drays and barges
and the smell and taste
of big red copper pennies
for the slot machines
in the Fun Palace

And tiny on Eden Quay
the missing Astor Cinema:

Where I saw (*He saw*)
I saw
The Wages of Fear
Ballad of a Soldier
The Cranes are Flying

355

Fanfan La Tulipe
Les Enfants du Paradis
Casque D'Or Golden Marie
flicker of shadows
of shadows

My breath tightens
along the river
Wind and gulls
May it not be lost
May it not be lost forever

Leland: PS From Yalta

For Lissadell read Leland
my dearest long-term-lea-land-by-the-sea
where you've so well touched shore
home free
and I still making for Astapovo

There was a house in Leeson Street
and they called it 33 ...
Keep it up for twenty years the poetry
Kavanagh's words to me
in your front room

Keep spinning spinning never stop
you told me then
as you've been spinning since dear love
with your trampoline and music –
just keep on buying those pianos

Dearcadh

after Eoin Mac Lochlainn's Exhibition

Shining orrery
Black helicopter
Turning to the sun

Stag beetle
Shellacked gondola
Patent leather

If I could find

Black polish
And the smell of it
Black lead

Black Eyes
And Moscow Nights
Distended pupils

the whisper

Soot on a wall
Burnt sugar
My friend the scorpion

Charred wood
Black bile
Black blood

that runs through this

Black cloth
Black leather breviaries
Black wings

The darkness
Of the pit
Beneath the lake

the making

Darkness
Dumb
In the back of the mouth

The black black
Water
Where there is no air

And There It Is: *Вот Там* ...

As I remembered it
Linz of the silent trams
That could so well knock down
An ageing gent
With ears unsure
And eyes grown faint

On the glide between
The Hauptplatz to
The Ursulines and Klosterhof
They pass up and down
Like busy toys
Rehearsing for Christmas

And the silence is lethal
Oiled and lethal as when
You have left yourself
Abandoned in a far-off place
And wait for a word
Or the touch of a breath

Dead Light: December

Tá sé fuar arsa an seanduine
Is é atá arsa Séimí
Fuar fuar
 —Seamus Ó Grianna, *Caisleán Óir*

i

I have been here before
In the long wet yellow winter
Strands of grass

And crows in the trees above:
Then too I felt like starting over
Unable to catch

The present moment:
Seeing that
There is no present moment

After all
No present language
Just the past and future

Travelling in opposite directions
Rushing further outwards
To the edge

And start of things:
That quick spasmodic clutch of urgency
Spilling

361

Into open ground
All blood and bone and hope
All past and future

All one and none:
And burning here an eager moment
Been and gone

The same: spat out to find
And drowning in
That ocean that we cannot enter

ii

Imperfect story of the Voyage
When time is bent
And calculation fails

Even in the daily
Present tense
That colluding social point

As near as we can come
To now:
To go to sleep at twenty one

And wake at sixty
Alone or with
Another head upon the pillow:

Not much comfort
For a stoic
I gCaisleán Óir or anywhere

Else but what there is
I'll take
Rise once more from the pit

And I who haven't been drunk
In thirty years
Can call to mind

Being on the road in Spain
At twenty-one: being
Young in Spain in Spanish boots

iii

My hands two yellow creatures
On the page
Like lizards hold the book

While those other poor bare creatures
Dip and thrust
Around the margins

Swaying and moaning
Gasping
Sucking licking faking

A hundred thousand times an hour
Like piston heads:
Spéir-bhean or *aisling*

Lena cam seang geal –
An tusa Helen nó Venus gleóite:
Ireland of the present times

A voice remembered
O flower of the amber locks?
Or the bare-breasted

Snake goddess of Crete
I found in the parlour book-case
Long ago in County Meath:

The stinging nettles
And the naked female satyr waiting
In the thistles in the field

Song

Air: Dicey Reilly, slowly

Rose from my bed to mend my head
And fumbled out the door
Into the street to find relief
As many times before
With one sleeve on and one shoe off
Astray in time direction lost
And the start of my ruin was rising early

Still searching for the Angel
I went walking through despair
And when we met she told me
That I lived in disrepair
It's clear said she you're sorely pressed
Out here again and half undressed
Oh the start of my ruin was rising early

I thought that life was love revealed
That everyone agreed
That no one there intended harm
Kind lilies of the field
Beneath my feet no stones of doubt
Until the tide of youth went out
When the start of my ruin was rising early

I learned the cost of what I'd lost
But learning comes too late
So little time for love or rhyme
With the Piper at the Gate

To wreak in full the banishment
Of all who don't put by the rent
And the start of my ruin was rising early

And thus the years have come undone
To leave me walking still
Along the docks and promenades
In the morning river chill
There's no going back I must go on
Each night and day pass through the dawn
For the start of my ruin was rising early

Clare Island

Quand irons-nous, par delà les grèves et les monts
—Arthur Rimbaud, *Saison En Enfer*

i

Deep in the unknown
empty quarter
of that country

There is a lake
and in the middle of the lake
there is an island

And in the middle
of the island
stands a mountain

And from its top
the oceans of the world
are visible:

We are less different
from each other
than islands from the land

ii

This is how we
came here
like the cormorant

Inhabiting two species
the water and
the stone walls on the mountain

Peruvian marks
of lazy-beds
stretched all across the countryside

Sailing out of Roonagh
a red queen and a white queen
dance across the bay

Coming midday
into harbour
with a thin moon overhead

iii

Strip away words
lesser words
and few

Seeing things
from nearer to the ground
to focus small:

Grains of salt
around the rock-pool
shell

Stone
flat sea and open sky
is vastness

Is silence
sound and vastness
of everything grown in

iv

Like fence-posts we stick up
on the horizon
figures masts and tower

Over and beyond
islands are like lakes inverted
upside down

The sea above
the giant hollow places
far beneath

My father told me
look at mountains paintings
upside down

Over there inside my head
still watching
light and shade on Minaun

v

When you walk around an island
you do not come back
to where you started out

This is the Imram
and the fact:
the day itself has changed

And light and time
the moving measure
of us all moved on

The ritual
of couples landing here
and setting out

At once
on bicycle and foot
to map the edges of this Ark

vi

The tower house is present
as the sea is
always present and the wind

That blows the county flags:
as sheep
as sea gulls up above the wind

And cloud and mountains
blue on grey on blue
all life: and signs of life

A shovel lying on the ground
a coal bag
underneath a bush

Blue clothes-pegs
paint tins
bags of sand cement and stones

vii

Children in the schoolyard
in the sun
girls and boys

With helmets hurleys:
a sliotar in his hand
the teacher

Is explaining all
the expertise
of poc and stance

Above the glittering sea
that stretches out
to Inishturk

And fuschia green and red
is everywhere
all Mayo red and green

viii

Please do not touch
the curraghs ...
the archetypal care

As Liam Brady heard
a woman say
in Connemara

Half a century ago: *a mhac*
ná bí
ag briseadh bád

Everything comes here
by hand
by sea and history

One way and another:
Terra
Marique Potens O Maille

ix

In the cloisters
of the monastery of Oliveto
there is

A Signorelli fresco
of the angels visiting in mufti
one woman

Cutting bread
another pouring wine or water
from a jug for them:

The stuff of day to day
unconsciously rehearsed
as this

The scene repeated here
a young girl
pouring tea into a cup

x

Sand in the breaking waves
stones talking
in the flow back undertow

The low-tide rolling talk
of stones
along the beach

And the one-eyed dog
who waits
all afternoon in hope

Of stone or stick
thrown in for him to fetch
clocks off goes home

I see him next day
hard at work
driving sheep down to the boat

xi

I saw that red-gold hair before
in Philip's tomb
in Macedon

Burning red-gold
oak branch diadem and filigree
of twigs and leaves

That living artistry of wind
and chance
that crosses time

Comes down to us
like amber
floating on the Baltic sea:

A woven beehive
and a sea-wise cloth
such wisdom Ariadne brought

xii

Standing at the end of Europe
by Grace O'Malley's grave
in the Atlantic

The sea-light
seeping through the stone and windows
the fading painted figures

On the walls and ceiling
reaffirm
the unseen acts of reverence repeated

That we apply
the sanctity we bring to things
are what survive:

These damaged boars and stags
still living here
that sleek elastic hound

xiii

Going the road from
sea to sea
where the valley rises up

Between
Knockmore and Knocknaveen
and a woman on her bike

Comes cycling from the sun
none but us both
in that stupendous space

And loneliness:
the simple endless moment
of being there

And nowhere else
and knowing it: and then to leave
a moment so inhabited

xiv

Arrival and departure
all going to and coming from
in the unending

Business
of ferrying
the present to the present:

We land and gravitate a while
disperse
take credit for the weather

The wooden benches
for the passer by
stare out to sea:

A line of great stone heads
we shade our eyes
looking out to where we were

xv

They do not come again
the flashing lines
these glancing

Points of contact
if we don't
quickly press them to the page

The moments when
each frame becomes another
then another:

Making now for Roonagh
one young woman
hands round sweets

The rolling sea is luminous
a young man spends the journey
looking back

From The Notebooks of Dr Jules Cotard (1840–1889)

Is that distorting glass
In the bathroom mirror?
No I don't believe so – Why?
When I looked just now
I didn't recognise myself:
I did not see someone else
But if I didn't know myself
Then who was it I saw?

There is no God or Devil
Said Mme Zero to her lover
I am dead these 40 years
Invisible before my time
Must live like this forever
An empty fairy-tale of ice
A solitary off-stage voice
And if that goes I will be lost
Water dripping on my arms
Not knowing where I've gone

As the first thing was the word
The end of everything
Is silence
The silence before the sound
And the silence after
And at the end of language

To go out like a candle
Amid owls and jackals
Or a paraffin lamp in darkness:
With the enormous silence
Full of inaudible music

From my father I inherited
A love of lonely places
Old graveyards
Empty parks and gardens
Canal banks railway lines
Country paths
The seashore in the morning:
The time my son and I
For five long days in Umbria
Saw not a single soul
Knew that we were dead
And taught the sheep
Upon the hill
Behind the house to sing

Confusion of airports
Anonymity of numbers
And in the forest
In the cool dark forest
The unreality of green:
In crowds to see and feel desire
To recognise it
To see it in a stranger's eyes:
Causes the blood to stop

Coagulate
Despite the physicality
The pumping of the heart

To be a locus only
That registers the passage
Of events: three figures
On a balcony in Mexico
A Famous Painter
A Famous Writer
A Famous Revolutionary
The accidental others in the picture
A young couple
Have not been identified:
Little Soselo loved flowers
Reached out to touch
And The Red Tsar learned to walk

And finally the brazen-calf
Automaton begins to speak:
Trifles prosecute – it roars –
Identity accelerates reflection
Mirror assures the image
And image worships mirror
In vein the nerves lust:
Will love shelve the fantasy?
The origin accesses memory
What good is this?
Why can memory not groan?

That We May Go On

Some of us are going to
Have problems
On the Last Day
With the resurrection of the flesh
Rising from the earth
Looking for teeth and foreskins
With elbows glued to ears
Our bones advancing
Backward like so much bric-à-brac

We'll have to disentangle
That: but what about the cells?
The universe of living cells
Exchanged
Those carbon miles of DNA
That we have wrapped around the world?

Tangential moments
Sending cells of light
Across the dark

I am thinking now of you
My 50-years-ago laid low
With eve-of-treatment nerves
Like Queen Titania
Played by Judi Dench
A whole midsummer and midwinter
Before a starlit audience:
And then tomorrow
When the chemicals will start again
The rude mechanicals

That keep you here a while
Our revels now are ended
But they're not –
Not this scenario
           and not
Before we hit the Place Maubert

Taken From Candide

Before he passed away becoming
In the process Pangloss Bán
Weighed down with honours
I spoke to him
About that Borges poem –
The unknown book
He would never reopen
The anonymous street in Buenos Aires
He would never walk again:
Such plank-in-reason moments
As being outside at night and falling
Into stars and ice and distance
That sudden clutching cold of emptiness –

There is some perfect other
That I shall never meet
Some word that I shall never say
Though being here at all depends on both

But from himself an airy gesture
    of distaste
As from the Inns of Court –
With too much certainty for doubt
His fine-drawn face closed shut
With centuries of common sense
Imperious behind him – the cloistered
Politics of working-through the possible:
His conscious ear half-turned away
A living Eclogue in himself I thought

And more fool I: come closing time
Among the tipsy sans culottes
I watched as he sailed up and out
Into the darkness of the night
Majestic as a bull to stud
Unerring heavy practiced
Skirting his way past Saturn Mars and Venus

Left-Handed Notes

I hear and I remember
How I was
The ghost of Quasimodo
Chuting hundred-lire pieces
Thirty years ago
From hand to hand
Gout-crippled in Siena ...
And what's that other sound
From the wood?
A bad-tempered turtle dove
You said?

When I am alone
I speak to silence
And my aperçus go unrecorded –

And memory is where I am
One-fingered memory
Poking round among the ruins
Seeing again how
The Gaelic bards were right
Retiring to an unlit place
The battened hold of a boat
For composition
With a flat stone on the stomach

I've been here for weeks now
Semi-seduto
Sleeping in three hour bursts
And the little corner
Top-left of the wooden shutters

Gouged out by an owl
Pins everything in place
My beacon in the early morning
A cobweb on the dawn
At night a portal to the universe
Is like a tooth the tongue
Keeps coming back to
A referential point of discipline
As this Tutorial
Strapped tight
To pull my shoulders back

As the body loosens
Moments of pain grow more intense
The gap between decision
And misdirected information
From the nerves
Widens into synapses
Of wires that do not touch:
The yard is full of pictures
On a level with my eyes
But I cannot wipe the dust away
To catch one clearly –
Enough that
Sunlight washes me with heat
As I walk slowly up and down
A Jesuit without a breviary
All things sacred
And profane
And slowly mending bone

An intelligence on sticks
Is what I have become
Cracked egg with legs

I have a plan for working out
The distance when I walk
I take a clothes-peg in my fist
From the clothesline
To the fence
Pin it there collect another
Twenty pegs a thousand metres
Dante pacing stanzas
In a single room in Florence

For years I have been conscious
Of the mockery of sounds
How pigeons here
Call out
In tones of purest Ranelagh
Fuck-off you fuck-off you
And then from the hill
Behind the house
Its Echo
Turning into stone
You're useless you're useless
With time the thought
Becomes less venomous
And now I simply acquiesce
Broken by a moving staircase
It means no more nor less
Than nightingales –
Those nightingales
I sometimes … hardly hear
Before I try to fall asleep
Dulled down with pills

You should have wheels
On that said Pelle

In the Port in Boston
Looking at my Samson bag
Stuffed solid as a haggis
You should have wheels on that
You know my dear
You're not a cowboy any more
The prairies in the phrase
Meant general absolution
In the concrete noonday Sun
And being thus absolved
Of everything for ever more
Three years later
I set carefree wheels and foot
To step
Mid-flight ascending
From Dormition all alone
Upon the scala mobile
In Fiumicino and hurtled
Down like Lucifer to Hell –
Breaking ribs and
Clavicle
But saving neck and skull

And what surprised me most
Was how a serious rush of guilt
Almost sexual
Possessed me
That same apportioning of blame
They teach us from the start
It was my fault all mine
And mine alone
That gravity had flung me down
That the escalator steel
Was unforgiving cruel

That I had lost control
And come to grief
That I had somehow
Done this insult to myself
As if I had not learned by now
Or having learned forgot
That life is all indifference
Of action and reaction
The single sperm
That gets there in the end
Is purposeful
And random:
Chance and meaningless

But still I have been waiting
For the fireflies those
Fantastic lovely architects
Of light – who build
When I am here
Manhattans out of space
And flying tiny sparks
Along the road at night
For me to walk through
In the dark
My geographical escapes
Among the insect life of Umbria
(Tell Jellinek from me
It works)
The noises and the starlit
Lovely dark – tonight
The nightingales are manic
In the cooler air
A parlement of foules
All open-throated trills

As forceful as the diva
Singing Turandot that August
Night in Macerata
Before the thunder:
The weather
Driving home with us
Across the
Appenines into the dawn

Where does the pain go
When it eases –
Like that fantastic sound
Into the Marche night?
How many angels and etcetera …
The shutter's broken louvres
Emphasise the light
Each morning as I wake
Edges jagged as my own
Five grinding broken ribs
And floating round
Inside my shoulder
Four dying pieces of mosaic
That were my collar bone

I heard but never saw
The bird that gnawed
Away the corner of the shutter
Athene's owl that landed
On the roof at night
A muffled sound
Like a Victorian burglar
The Hoxton Creeper
Quick and crude enough
And down to business

Lifting up the tiles to reach
The nestling sparrows underneath
Nor did I ever see a stim
Of any raven of ill-omen
Flying high above me
To the staircase –
Who ever knows
The signals of their own demise
Before
The ticking bomb explodes:
The ancient woman
In the the stream beside the road
Who washes
Bloodstained clothes

Three weeks later
And the pain starts letting go
Like ice unclenching
At the end of winter
Walking up and down the yard
I'm looking further outwards
Past the clothes-pegs
Forming and reforming
Quantum codes
Of maths and music
Red and white
In zig-zag on the fence
And past the donkey path
I've worn away – my
Mulish three mile daily dance
Of reconnection with myself

And looking outwards see again
The ruined house

Across the way – (the one
That bollox said he'd buy
Ex-British Army yes
And would-be S.A.S.
At least it didn't come to that) –
Its ruined permanence
Invincible
                and further still
Just there
And always there
The marvellous trees
The marvellous clouds

And the single
Hanging hawk upon the wind

May / June 2009

Mending: May 2009

Slow motion snow
Again the drifting poplar seeds
Across the valley

Suddenly so beautiful
The May-green hazels
And the quince

Mysterious
And around the corner that
Wild olive that we thought was dead

Blood flows
In this repeated spontaneity
Fresh growth new bone

Snake Reprise

I walked again to the German house
Up past the walnut tree
With the concrete posts
Like seats beneath –
Hieronymo to the hazel-wood
The usual mist
With nothing changed and nothing the same

The lucerne had overnight become
An olive grove
The house still tightly barred and shut
The barbed wire gone
That had been stretched across for a gate
There was no one there
No one there at all
But for a formal pair
Of high-heeled shoes on the door step

In the middle of the day
With no one there
Nothing lasts unchained said the porcupine
But the same
Never-quite-finished sunlight
Turning around and around like a clock
In the noonday silence
Of cicadas birds and childen's laughter

The trick is to assemble the mise-en-scène
One piece at a time
One foot before another –
The high-heeled shoes on the step

The empty pulsing snakeskin
Trembling in the air
The rusty wire drawing blood
And the urgency of what was there before
What might have been
Butterflies that come and go
Between the red-hot-poker and the rose

But you were there you were there
Caws the crow from the wood
No no I'm a stranger here
Sings the nightingale on the gate-post
All of us are
All of us are
Says the worker bee in the lavender

Easter Saturday 2010

Hoxton Square on a sunny afternoon
And everything has been updated
Caffè Latte in Shoreditch Station
Far from Jeannie Robertson
In Hackney – the heartache
Of those preludes and romances

Things are better than they were
And truth to tell
I don't need them now at all –
The old addictions
All that time and duty spent
In a distant reckless country

Better to be a living dinosaur
The Satnav uttering directions
Tomorrow maybe
We'll take a trip to Brighton – but when
I leave for home I'll hear
Drums beating softly in the distance

The Welder Embracing Silence

I have lost the striking
Of the arc he said
Stepping back into the light
I have lost the contact
Between hand and eye

The contact between
Sound and tongue remains:
Between the image
And the brain:
But I have lost the contact

Between what I see
And what I know I am:
The thin-skinned
Living touch is gone
The cunning of the hand

Blessed Thomas Of Prague

Poor Thomas of Prague arrived in Sydney
Tired and weary
Carrying an empty plastic bag
Wearing a suit gone at the knees

When he got as far as Immigration
He lowered his trousers
And adjusted himself
Said the Customs Inspector

A pensioner with 500 dollars
And little English
Overweight and bemused
Who wanted to see Hyde Park

Confused said the next Inspector
In the chain of command –
Except when he spoke in Czech
When he sounded just like anyone else

Tired and adrift
With hypothetical things to do
But no more than the rest of us
Could Thomas fully explain himself

Confused said the Chief Inspector
The man's a joke
He has insufficient money and
Has quantities of soil between his toes

Hosed down in the shower
Dressed once more in his baggy suit
They spun him around and flew him back
Still talking of seeing Hyde Park

Maenads

for Pelle Lowe

It is dark and there is a smell
Of pines as always
When the summer heat is over
After rain the sun is back

And symbols have become
The thing itself – this is the south
Where great matters
Are discussed in doorways

On the lower level of the parking lot
I was talking to myself
Reading circles in the dust
When the crash occurred:

Today I saw Ms Jackie Smith
Horned and elegant
Walking before me in Rapallo –
Yesterday in Po' Bandino

Falling down from the sky
Like those giant sunlit
Raindrops in September
With a couple of metres in between

Tumbling down from the hills
She was:
Head over heels and laughing
Wrestling with a mountain lion

Ice Burning: St Sebald

Word has it on the street
That he was devious
Louche they said and furbo
Given to hyperbole
Slick tricks and sleight of hand

Sneaking photos of the ceiling
In San Pantalon
Or the time at Regensburg
He crossed the Danube
On his outspread cloak

(Though not such a feat
When you think
Of Irish and Breton Saints
Sailing their Celtic Sea
In thick stone boats ...)

And then the shattered chalice
He made whole
The myriad shards of glass
Rejoining on the tiles
Impelled by an act of will

And the strange performance
In the wheelwright's
With no kindling twigs to hand
Cajoling the fire alight
With icicles for sticks

(I think he maybe just forgot
To bring the kindling in
The night before
And was unwilling now
To traipse outside in snow)

All of us have done
A thousand such impossible things
Extempore and unrehearsed
Without smoke and daggers
Or second thoughts

On an Umbrian road I met
An ostrich and two llamas
Quietly grazing the long acre
While new-felled poplars lay nearby
Beached like whales

Is not this too
A wonderment and curious –
That we buy tickets for the miracle
As we buy tickets
To the travelling circus

Istanbul Arrival

At Kabatas Pier
He steps ashore from Asia
Carrying lilies

In The Light Of Whipple's Moon

My first time travelling
With Ms Jackie Smith
She had but lately changed
Become a silver birch
From being a silver beech

On six-inch high stillettos
Containing within her
A continent of knowledge
And she a fleet of bark canoes
To sail the waters

Next I saw her in midwinter
In the mountains
Standing with open arms
And upthrust branches
Eloquent against the sky

In what she called
Her stance for taking off
And where are we aiming for
I asked what next? Still
Travelling light enough

To fly through light itself
She said – to get from here
To the nearest star
Or near enough to touch
It starts with a ten-day walk

Leaving the *case sparse*
Scattered houses on your left
Over the land of olives
Across the icy lake of moons
To reach the Scattered Disc

But first you have to learn
Perhaps by telescope
The names and constellations
Of vanished peoples
In the maproom of the Doge

All that Magnificence
Scrolled dolphins reading books
And Chiron with a dorsal fin
Turned arabesque
Ambiguous below the waist

Remember what she said
The Delphic priestess on the rock
The words before she struck
The downward stroke
That left you broken up

Once more you must move on
Align the omphalos
Just play it as it lays
And after that – who knows?
The centre of the universe?

In May The Park And Me Revisited

The dropouts in the park
Are drinking Bud and Efes
I read the bottle caps
And pull-off tags from cans
Among thin plastic tubes
And tell-tale roaches
                            May
Green is all about
And the community of carp
The grey friars of the lake
Are one with children
And their watchers
And all the levels in between
                            And I
With those delusive ghosts
Of loneliness and failure
All the empty spaces of the years
Left unredeemed
And all the missing people
Myself among them
                            When
Suddenly being here at all
Amid the sad detritus
Of bottle caps and memories
Beneath my feet
It somehow all seems *yet* –
Too beautiful to leave

Unfolding

for Pearse Hutchinson 1927-2012

The heron's marvellous
unfolding
a surprising
practical effrontery
in the flat light
around the pond
this afternoon
unfolding like a kite
and flying off

*('sometimes he does just that
other times he just does that')*

An old man stranded
like a stork
on a chimney pot
room
   breathing
      Bach
and rich tea biscuits
the flutter of a piece
of paper
    unfolding

holding the moment tight

We Have Given Up On Hills

I have given up on hills
but I can walk forever on the flat
I thought and tried
although suspecting that
more things are settled
over chat
than I could manage
in a three day march

These days I find my feet
in Superquinn
preoccupied among the herons
standing in the aisles
watchful poised intent
                    about to ...
always on the point of ...
following through
the frozen moment into flight

Or taking heron-hops
across the lake –
like Gene Kelly as D'Artagnan
avoiding Richelieu's
ducks and gulls
until we're hardly here at all
or there
among the passers by
strollers children dogs and lumps of bread

Brief flapping walks
with leather wings extended
in the January dark:
two herons and myself
despite good sense
still holding on
maintaining flesh and feather:
all downhill from here
it looks
but downhill we can walk forever

NOTES

'Lazarus In Fade Street' (p. 79) was written in the contentious atmosphere of the 1986 Divorce Referendum, during which Alice Glenn, ultra-conservative Fine Gael T.D., said that women voting for Divorce were like turkeys voting for Christmas; Padraig Flynn, Fiannna Fáil T.D., declared fervently for The Family.

'Fire And Snow And Carnevale' (p. 158) was adapted by Brendan Graham and made into the song, 'Winter Fire And Snow', first issued as CD in 1995 with Katie McMahon and Anuna, and subsequently recorded by Benita Hill, Eimear Quinn and many others.

The Ranelagh Gardens/apuntos sin titulos collaboration with the composer Benjamin Dwyer (first performed in the Mostly Modern series in the Bank of Ireland, College Green, Dublin, in February 2003) began in 2002. The public park in Ranelagh became the genesis of the poem (p. 276) and of the title. A CD, *In The Ranelagh Gardens,* music and poetry, was issued in 2005.

On June 8th 2002, Richard Hartshorne performed the Six Solo Suites by Bach, at the Verbal Arts Centre in Derry, on the double bass. My sequence (p. 289) arose initially out of that event. Poem and music together have been performed in the U.S. and Canada.

'Kavanagh In Umbria' (p. 325) and 'Hadewijch' (p. 337) were my contribution in two separate collaborations with artist Constance Short, in 2004 and 2005).

The Clare Island poems (p. 367) grew out of a commission to supply text for a book of photographs of the Island, *(This time, this place,* Mayo Co. Council 2007), taken by photographer Jim Vaughan (Mayo Artist Panel 2005/2006) and by the people of the Island themselves.

Lightning Source UK Ltd.
Milton Keynes UK
UKHW010655300920
370782UK00001B/23